Theodore Charles Gambrall

Church Life in colonial Maryland

Theodore Charles Gambrall

Church Life in colonial Maryland

ISBN/EAN: 9783337153687

Printed in Europe, USA, Canada, Australia, Japan

Cover: Foto ©ninafisch / pixelio.de

More available books at **www.hansebooks.com**

COLONIAL MARYLAND,

—— BY ——

REV. THEODORE C. GAMBRALL, A. M.

BALTIMORE:
GEORGE LYCETT,
No. 44 LEXINGTON STREET,
1885.

TO MY FRIENDS,

THE PARISHIONERS OF ST. JAMES' PARISH, ANNE ARUN-
DEL COUNTY, MARYLAND,

THIS VOLUME IS AFFECTIONATELY INSCRIBED, IN RECOG-
NITION OF THEIR MANY MARKS OF KINDNESS
SHOWN THROUGH MANY YEARS.

T. C. G.

MAY 1ST, 1885.

PREFACE.

The author, in offering this volume to the consideration of the public, does not desire that it shall be looked upon as a history of the Church in Maryland through the period which it covers, but rather as one among many aids to the writing of that history which is yet to be. He is aware of the existence of a considerable body of materials which he has not been able to utilize, and he has been made very conscious through all his labor in this connection, that both the engrossing nature of his parochial duties and the remoteness of his residence from all literary centers, would render him unfit for the ambitious plan of the history of the church in this province. The title of the work expresses its object, *Church Life in Colonial Maryland*; for the writer's purpose has been, by the blending of parochial records with documentary and other evidence of a more general character, along with a continuous glance at the world outside the colony, to give as near as may be, both a peculiar and also a relative insight into the condition of the Church of our fathers. How far he has succeeded in this purpose he must leave it to others to determine.

The author feels, however, that he has some special qualifications for this work. A Maryland Churchman by birth, he is proud of her traditions, and proud of her eminent position. He also feels the heartiest sympathy with that tone of Churchmanship which permeates all parts of the commonwealth, which had its origin in those days when the Church was *the Church* in the minds and mouths of all, when dissent was a small faction worshipping in its chapels, and when the parson was the generally accepted presentation of Christ's duly ordained minister. That is Maryland Churchmanship; and it has been fostered and preserved through all the older rural districts of Maryland, where the old temples still stand, and where the children of a long line of fathers still occupy the soil.

Another qualification also, he feels that he has in being the rector of one of the first parishes in Maryland; first, principally because it was created along with those that were laid out under the earliest act of establishment; first, because from that earlier day it has been blessed, almost without exception, with a long line of ministers who have furthered the kingdom and done no dishonor to their holy calling, the parish thus enjoying an even life of high tenor; first, because those who worship within its sanctuary, love the Holy Name, and are thankful for their Churchly inheritance; and among the first, because though resources have been severely crippled, and numbers sadly reduced by untoward circumstances, their is a willingness to help build up Zion, to repair the waste places, to make the desert rejoice and blossom as the rose.

Presenting, therefore his claims for attention, he prays for consideration, and trusts that the effect of his labor may be to correct misapprehension, and to reveal to many the true historical position of their church in this diocese, fostering thereby their zeal in its behalf.

CHAPTER I.

THE CHURCH BEFORE 1692.

INTRODUCTORY.

The history of a parish in Maryland cannot properly go back beyond the year 1692 when the first act of the Colonial assembly was passed for the establishment of the church of England in the now royal province. Still it would be erroneous to suppose that there had been no existence of the church in the colony before. Rather the evidences are various that from the foundation of the colony there had been many members of that church among the settlers, some of them very influential, while also in the Virginia settlement on Kent Island, which had been established in 1629, years before Lord Baltimore's emigrants had arrived in the colony, the church of England services were conducted by a duly ordained minister. Lord Baltimore's endeavors had been strenuous to secure a large body of colonists, as the "Account" published with the Father White papers shows, and his invitation was in no way limited to the members of his own church, as in the nature of things it could not have been.

The existence of this Protestant element also soon began to show itself, for though we do not have any early notice of a duly established congregation ministered to by a clergyman, we find Protestants assembling together for mutual edification, as in the case of the servants of Cornwallis in 1638; while also in 1642 we find the small colony disturbed by an attempt to deprive certain "Protestant Catholics" of the use of their chapel and to despoil them of the books of the same, a term of designation which Bozman, the chief historian of that period, thinks can only mean members of the Church of England. Indeed the most recent light thrown upon the history of that time, that from the Jesuit Fathers, whose records in the matter are now in hand, shows that beyond all question from the beginning the Protestants were in the majority; the provincial, Henry Moore, writing to Rome in 1642, saying "The affair was surrounded with many and great difficulties, for in leading the colony to Maryland, by far the greater part was heretics." Also we are told by the same authority that the assembly which met in 1638, in which all the freemen could be present either personally or by proxies, "was composed with few exceptions of heretics;" of whom probably the larger part were of the Church of England, seeing that persons of Puritan views who would seek an asylum, would rather prefer the northern colonies where everything was conducted so much more to their liking. Consistent only with this fact of the majority of the colonists being Protestants, is the progress of things from the year 1648. For though up to this time Lord Baltimore had consulted his private preferences in choosing members of his church for the offices of the colony, yet now we find him appointing a Protestant governor and a Protestant council, with also a Protestant secretary of State; while also we find the embodiment of the new feature of general toleration in the oath of office, both of the governor and council, with particular definiteness in the former in favor of Roman Catholics; and the enactment by the assembly, on presentation by the Proprietary, of what is entitled an Act concerning Religion (1649) in which toleration is provided for all believers.

These things confirm the previous evidence, if any confirmation were necessary. Maryland continued to be a refuge for Roman Catholics. Roman priests, especially the Jesuit Fathers, continued to be very active, many being sent over to the colony from time to time, though sometimes giving great trouble to the authorities from the extravagance of their pretensions. All the way along through the whole colonial history members of this church ever wore a threatening aspect to the minds of all Protestants, and jealousy of them gave a war cry that could excite the fiercest passions. Their numbers were always such as to make them a force and sometimes a terror; and in the many risings of the people during the first fifty-five years of the colony, dread of them was a largely prevailing cause of fear.

In 1656 one of Lord Baltimore's friends, Hammond, writing in his behalf, states that at that time the population of the colony was composed of Conformists, non-Conformists, and a few Papists, the first in which catalogue being members

of the Church of England. The First minister
of this church as far is known (not including the
one previously settled on Kent Island) came into
the colony about 1650, with his wife and
daughters, and engaged in ministerial labors.
The evidences, however, are that he was compelled to seek subsistence in part from sources other
than the offerings of the people, a fact that has
always held, not only in new countries, but in
those where the population is sparse. The support and prosperity of the church in rural districts,
have always been dependent upon some form of
endowment or external aid. Lord Baltimore, in
defending himself from charges made in 1676,
asserted that the clergy then in the province
had each of them a plantation, which probably
they had entered and possessed on the same terms
as the other private individuals. For as yet
there were no parishes in existence, and besides,
there was extreme jealousy felt against church
or other corporations acquiring property, and it
was forbidden without special license obtained from the Lord Proprietary. The
statute of Mortmain was made to bear on the
matter, the anxiety of Lord Baltimore and
the colonial authorities being chiefly excited by
the conduct of the Jesuits who took up immense
tracts of land for their society, though it was
held for them and was taken up in the name of
private individuals. They still hold a large portion of this their former possession. Altogether
at this time their relations in the colony were exceedingly strained, their assumptions of prerogative being very extravagant, even to the
point of independence of lay jurisdiction. Their

own authorities in England disapproved of their presumption, and Lord Baltimore, by consistency and resolution, sustained as he was by members of his own church, finally succeeded in maintaining his rights against their unwarrantable encroachments.

The facilities, however, for acquiring an estate in the province were so great that no one needed to suffer. For according to the conditions of plantation published by Lord Baltimore in 1636, after the year 1635 one thousand acres of land might be held for a yearly rental of twenty shillings, payable in the commodities of the province, and fifty acres for twelve pence, land being granted to applicants according to the number of the laborers brought into the colony. Under these conditions any minister could secure for himself a personal estate, and thus be guaranteed a maintenance. We are told, however, of two endowments that were created about the year 1676, one in Baltimore county and one in St. Mary's, in the latter case the corporation of the county being made the custodian of the fund. The clergy of the church began now to increase in numbers. For in 1676, in the answer above noted, we find Lord Baltimore declaring that there were four in the colony; a small number for the vast amount of work to be done. How far these were an honor to the church or efficacious for its beneficent purposes is a question; for of two of those, probably included in the four, John Coode and John Yeo, the history is, that the former was afterwards convicted of atheism and blasphemy, and that the latter was, to say the least of him, a turbulent man. There began now also a demand for ministers. In 1676 the latter of the above parties represented to the Archbishop of Canterbury in the strongest language, the great need of the colony for a duly provided for ministry to prevent the falling away of many churchmen to Popery, Quakerism or fanaticism, and to control the wide spread disregard of the ordinances of religion and of the proprieties of morality. He describes the colony as a Sodom of uncleanness and a pest house of iniquity. Nor was this the only demand for Church of England Clergymen. For in the year 1685 we find Mary Taney, wife of the sheriff of Calvert Co., and ancestress of the late Chief Justice of the United States, addressing a letter to the Archbishop of Canterbury, in which she pleads for means to erect a church and in part to support a minister, founding her plea upon her anxiety for her own family's welfare and that of her neighbors, dreading less they might otherwise be condemned to infidelity or apostasy. She had previously petitioned Charles the II for relief, who had sent over a minister, together with a number of Bibles and other church books, and also in this case her petition was received with favor and a clergyman sent over. Nor were her anxieties and those of Mr. Yeo and others groundless; for in the reports of the Jesuit Fathers through this period we find as the fruit of their labors seventy brought over to their church in 1672, in 1673 twenty-eight, in 1674 thirty-four, while there was also a mission carried on by the order of St. Francis.

The times of trouble were now, however, setting in upon the colony, religious matters being the great disturbing cause. The ferment that had been created in England by the report of a Popish plot, in which Titus Oates was the chief agitator, and used by such men as the Earl of Shaftesbury as a tool for political ends, spread also to the colony, and under Fendall and Coode the "No-Popery" cry excited a revolt in 1681. This was successfully quelled, but as the home country continued to be in a state of doubt and anxiety about the Protestant religion, the people not believing in Charles the Second's faithfulness to the Church, and knowing that his prospective successor, afterwards James the Second, was an avowed papist, so the province of Maryland was disturbed; the more particularly so, because Lord Baltimore was a member of the Roman Church. This was a natural cause for suspicion and alarm throughout all this period when the pretensions of the Roman Church to the right of interfering with states, were so much more avowed than now, and when temporal rulers could be found, under blind religious zeal, to proceed to such extremities as that of the Revocation of the Edict of Nantes with its fearfully ruinous consequences; and when the recollections of the horrible excesses of the thirty years war had not passed from the memories of living men, and when the echoes of the voice of Cromwell were still heard amongst the Alps shielding the hunted Waldensians from the blast of papal fury. Lord Baltimore, neither Cecilias nor Charles, deserved the suspicion; for both were liberal minded men, and both of them received from the Assembly of the province, testimonials of confidence and esteem, the former in 1671 and 1672, and the latter in 1676, 1682 and 1688. Still prejudices are generally ungovernable and suspicions incapable of entire restraint, and the dread of popery and of the effect of its teachings was in the very atmosphere of that time. In 1684 the Proprietary was ordered to put all offices in the hands of Protestants, though he showed the king that all the most important offices were in their hands already, and especially such offices as controlled the military establishment of the colony.

In 1681 the population numbered over 20,000, and according to an estimate at the time there were thirty Protestants to one Papist, a disproportion that might be supposed sufficient to give assurance to the majority. Lord Baltimore's deputies, however, managed, by some peculiar gift, to excite the anxieties of this body, already sensitive enough, so that when William of Orange was reported about to invade England, the fear of the people was that Maryland was to be placed in antagonism to this movement, which was felt to be, in the colony as well as in Great Britain, the only thing that could preserve the religion and liberties of·the country. For the deputies of Lord Baltimore not only failed to proclaim the joint sovereigns when they were raised to the throne, but previously had put the colony in a state of defense by collecting arms and other materials of war, as if to resist any attempt that might be made to reduce the province to the new obedience. "No Popery" therefore again rang forth as a cry, an association was formed, the citizens were called upon to take up arms, the deputies were dispossessed of their authority, a convention was assembled, and a petition and address justifying their proceedings were drawn up and presented to the king.

This was the Protestant Revolution whose object was, as stated by its friends, "The defense of the Protestant Religion, and the asserting the right of king William and queen Mary to the province of Maryland and all the English dominions." The convention, when it assembled in 1689, made many charges against the management of the colony, alleging excessive Jesuit influence over the officers administering the government, that the churches were all appropriated to the use of the Popish idolatary, and that under the permission or connivance of the goverment, murders and outrages of all kinds were perpetrated by the Papists upon the Protestants. They charged an arbitrary exercise of power against the Proprietary and that he had ignored, as far as possible, the sovereignty possessed by the crown, allegiance to the Proprietary being alone required in the colony. And they declared themselves discharged from all fidelity to the chief magistrates of the province because they had endeavored to deprive them of their lives, property and liberties, which they were bound to protect.

The King of course listened to all this, and the consequence was that Lord Baltimore was deprived of the functions of government, of which he remained disinherited for over twenty-five years, till 1715, and the colony was erected into a Royal province, with writs running in the King's name, and the governor and other officers appointed by his authority. The private rights, however, of Lord Baltimore were continued to him, together with his income from the land, whether his own extensive manors or the quit-rents due him from the settlers. He was the private owner of the whole domain. The prerogatives and emoluments of office he was stripped of, the excessive sensitiveness of the people rendering it impolitic, if not extremely dangerous to leave authority in his hands or to force back upon the citizens an administration which they had so forcibly disallowed. The year before the final rupture the President of the Assembly had openly drawn a picture of the prevailing immorality of the colony in respect of drunkenness, adultery, Sabbath breaking and swearing, that, having the endorsement of the lower house, shows that Lord Baltimore's influence in the administration of the colony had not been in the highest degree successful, and that radical measures had now become necessary. The establishment afterwards sprang into existence in answer to that need as the one thing most likely to prove efficacious; and doubtless it did so in an eminent degree, for from the beginning, in addition to the silent influence of the church, we find its authorities doing all in their power under the law to suppress immorality.

CHAPTER II.

THE ESTABLISHMENT OF THE CHURCH.

Under the Royal government of the colony the second act of the first assembly, convened in 1692, was that providing for the establishment of the Church of England, under which functions and prerogatives were given the said church endowing it with great and exclusive privileges. Nor are we to be surprised at such a measure; for the establishment of the church was looked upon throughout the world as legitimate and proper, such ideas coming down unquestioned from the remotest Christian antiquity. And even among the barbarians, as well as among the heathen of civilized states, it appeared to the rulers of kingdoms, with their generally arbitary power, to be only proper that they should provide for the support of religion, and in various ways control and direct its ministrations. Men had not yet outgrown this notion, and so during the period of the Commonwealth in England the Presbyterian church was established, and in New England, and in New York after a manner, as well as in Virginia and the more southern colonies, establishments were now the rule. There is no great wonder, therefore, that the colonists in Maryland proceeded to this step, in as much also as it appeared to them to be the only means to ends they fondly desired, the restraint of the Roman Catholic Church and the correction and improvement of the morals of the colony. For one of the assigned causes for their overthrow of the Proprietary's authority was the influence the Jesuits were able to wield in the government of the colony, a cause for alarm which may or may not have existed. One thing the people knew, the Roman priests were exceedingly energetic; and to counteract their influence, on the one side, as they won away Protestants in the dearth of spiritual ministration, and on the other, to save the people from the depths of immorality, into which from the same cause they were falling, provision was made under law by the unanimous voice of the representatives of the inhabitants, for the support of a Protestant ministry; and the Church of England was chosen because it had the affections and loyalty of by far the largest part of the people of the colony. All differences were sunk in the Assembly under the sense of a great constraining necessity.

Much has been said about the ingratitude of this act and the consequent repression of the Roman Catholics, by whom, as is alleged, great liberality had formerly been shown; and certainly the thing is against all our present American notions. But the whole matter of the toleration secured in 1649, and what motives may have impelled the then Proprietary to lay it before the Assembly, are too fully presented to us now to justify any further talk about Protes tant ingratitude. For as we have seen, there is the best evidence that the Protestants were in a majority in the very first body of emigrants, a preponderance in strength which they always preserved; and any toleration that had ever been in the colony to this time had rather been by them than of them. The act must be looked at in the leading question of how far an establishment is ever justifiable. The Roman Catholics had been tolerated down this far in Maryland history. Consideration for them was opposed by the English ideas of that day. They dared not have established their own church, even had they had the power, or in any way have repressed persons of the Protestant faith. Lord Baltimore ever felt the force of this, and was earnest to impress upon the powers at home, that Roman Catholic as he was, and associated with the Jesuits as he was, equal liberties were enjoyed by all. A royal proclamation or an act of Parliament could at any time have deprived him of power in the case; as was done in the days of Cromwell, and again when Charles II. directed him to put all offices in the hands of Protestants, and finally when he was deprived of all government jurisdiction at the time of the Protestant Revolution. Also in the days of James II. the writ of *quo warranto* sued out by his royal majesty, made not only Lord Baltimore tremble, but the holders of many other charters besides. There was no ingratitude at all in the case. Neither Lord Baltimore nor his church ever had any power to establish their form of religion or to disfranchise other bodies than their own: and had they had the power they would not for a moment have dared to exercise it. The thunders of royal wrath and Parliamentary indignation would have overwhelmed the attempt in an instant. There was no ingratitude in the case; while we can sympathize with the colonists in their laying hold on the only available means of repressing a faction whose extravagant pretensions had, even in Maryland, given so much trouble to Lord Baltimore in the past, and whose principles had brought such trouble and mischief upon the world. For it was only seven year before this that Louis XIV. had revoked the Edict of Nantes which wrought intolerable and widespread ruin upon hundreds of thousands of Huguenots, depriving them in many instances of life and in almost all of property, and taking away rights dearer than life or property. It was the personal act of the king indeed, but received the approval both of the country and the church. It was at this time also that James the Second's conduct manifested all the qualities that the Roman Church might tolerate, violating his promises to maintain the Church of England, introducing the rites and customs of the Roman Communion, endeavoring to put places of trust and power in the hands of the members of that profession, seeking to ride down all law by suspending, by edict, every statute that might impede his will, and imprisoning the best and most exalted men of the realm whose faithful loyalty as citizens and ministers of the gospel prevented them from becoming the weak and pliable instruments for his tyrannical and arbitrary purposes. These things we must remember; nor can we forget the great agitation concerning the Popish Plot, which though granted, as we now see it, to have been a marvelous extravagance, still had some ground to rest on, and was firmly believed in by almost every one of that day.

Because of these things we can sympathize with the colonists of that time, and the more so when we recollect what the pretensions of the Roman communion were in regard to civil rulers and what had been attempted against the liberties of England in the days both of James I. and of Elizabeth, and that there was no place in Europe where the Roman Church was in the ascendency, where there was any toleration of divergent opinions. The mountains of the south of France were now ringing with the cries of the Camisards, struggling heroically against fearful odds for home and liberty and life, and the brutality of the house of Savoy, shown in the interests of religion, had not been forgotten. The true picture of the times was fearfully vivid to the minds of Maryland men at that period. With our American notions in this nineteenth century we disapprove of establishments altogether, and certainly such exclusive ones as that attempted in 1692. But the men of the seventeenth century were wise in their generation. They were educated by the circumstances of their day. Only the times have changed and we are changed with them.

The colonists, however, did not immediately succeed in their attempt. The law was not approved by the home government, which was neccessary now for its final validity, as in former days the approval of the Proprietary had been necessary. The cause of this non-approval was that the king regarded it as too exclusive; for brought up with his liberal Dutch notions he was far in advance of most persons in his day. Again and again was the law enacted with modifications, but as often rejected, until the year 1702, when Dr. Bray, the great friend of Maryland, and commissary, having returned to England, obtained permission to have an acceptable law drawn up, with the assurance that having been duly passed by the colonial Assembly it should stand approved. It was done, and in that year the Church of England was finally established in Maryland. The great hindrance all along had been the difficulty raised chiefly by the Quakers, though the Roman Catholics also exerted quietly some influence. The true position of the former had come now to be better understood, and the days of their persecution were over; so that the king confirmed the Maryland act with these words, "Have the Quakers the benefit of a toleration? Let the established church have an established maintenance." To the north of Maryland there had been granted to William Penn an extensive tract, on which many of his co-religionists were settled, and over which he had established a provincial government. Also by the toleration act passed in England in 1689 the Friends were granted freedom of worship.

That they should oppose, therefore, the act of establishment that would restrict their liberties was only natural, especially as now they formed a very considerable portion of the population, reckoned at this time at one-twelfth, among whom were included some of the most intelligent and thrifty citizens of the province. This is proven by various circumstances, as by the names of the persons who were members of the meeting, by the influence they exerted with the authorities, by their readiness and boldness in discussion, and by their threat to prosecute any priest or magistrate who should marry any Quaker children without their parents' or guardians' consent. This was done at a yearly meeting held in 1688, and of itself shows how secure they felt themselves to be. Their opposition we have seen was influential, but it was not finally effectual; for the king was content to secure for them the toleration of their separate assemblages, while they were required, along with all other persons, to contribute according to law to the support of the established church. For the act as finally passed, provided that the church of England should be established, and that for its support there should be levied annually a tax of forty pounds of tobacco per poll upon all the taxables of the colony; to be collected by the sheriff. The appointment of ministers to parishes was to be by the governor without appeal, induction being in his hands; the minister was to keep and provide for a clerk out of his income. Other sections of the law regarded marriages, and a table declaring who might marry was to be set up in the Churches. Only a minister could marry when there was one resident, his fee being five shillings sterling. The number of vestrymen was set at six at the least, two to be dropped every year. By a subsequent law in 1730 the two eldest in office were to be dropped and not to be liable again for three years. The minister was also a vestryman. A register of births, marriages and burials was to be kept, and by several clauses of the law the vestry was required to meet on a certain day in each month, the time fixed once for all "to prevent surprise." Provision was made for the current expenses of the parish, to be levied by the county courts. Persons refusing to become wardens were fined one thousand pounds of tobacco, to go to the king, a stronger assurance that the fine would be collected. No minister could hold more than two parishes, nor could he hold them without the consent of the vestries of both and the appointment of the ordinary. The vestry had the power of appointing lay readers during a vacancy, who were to take the oaths with which every office was surrounded in those days. The lay readers received compensation. A vestryman could be removed if he neglected his duties, and parishioners had the right to inspect the vestry books and to appeal to the governor and council against vestry acts. By the twenty-first section of the law Quakers and other dissenters were to have the benefit of the toleration act, while their places of worship were required to be reported and a register of them kept. It will be observed that persons refusing to serve as wardens were to be fined, while there was no such provision covering the case of persons elected to the vestry. The duties of the wardens were in some degree the more onerous, they being conservators of the peace about the church. And so compulsion in their case was felt to be necessary. It was rather taken for granted that a man elected vestryman, would serve because of the honor of the office, and would attend to his duties. If he did not he was to be disgraced by dismissal. It was found, however, that this law would not work, and by an act of 1730, the vestrymen were also subjected to fine, to be recovered by process before a justice of the peace, one half to go to the church and the other half to the informer. Dissenters also were eligible to the office of vestrymen, as was declared by order of the Governor and Council in 1751, Piscataway parish having refused to qualify one who had been elected. This act was passed at a time of extreme agitation in the colony concerning church matters. In 1706 provision, additional to that in the law, was made for the protection of Quakers and other Dissenters, by the passage of the English Act of Toleration; though some think, not with good intent, but because of the pains and penalties attached. For the whole English world then knew very little of religious liberty. Toleration, privilege, was granted; though often more as a political necessity than for any other reason. The right to say what persons should believe, and that they should believe something, was supposed to reside in the powers that be; and so Unitarians as well as Roman Catholics were excepted from the public grace bestowed, a grace that could at any time, according to the theory, be recalled. Toleration proved to be, however, the embryotic condition out of which has been developed by fostering circumstances, the full grown man of religious liberty, at least in the Protestant world.

It may be advisable here to review for a

moment the relation of the province of Maryland to the home country, though what may be said of Maryland could generally be said of the other colonies. A law of England was not binding in the colonies unless it was expressly adopted there, or unless it was made for the colonies, as the Navigation Acts were, so that while persecution raged in England against all the various forms of dissent from the days of the settlement of Maryland, and cruel laws were passed for the purpose of repressing such dissenters, in New England, in New York, in New Jersey and Pennsylvania, and in Maryland, there were to be found laws in every way contradictory of the English statutes. The freest asylums were provided in the New World for those who by the Test, Conventicle and similar acts, were debarred all the rights of religious freedom. And so the Toleration Act had to be passed by the Assembly of Maryland before it could become a law. On the other hand laws passed by the colonial legislature had to be approved by the King, or afterwards by the Proprietary, before they could become operative, as was the case with the act of establishment; though a law passed by the assembly went into effect immediately upon its passage and was regarded as binding until it was disapproved by the superior authority. And so the act of 1692 was carried out, the province laid out into parishes, other laws passed laying duties upon vestrymen, ministers settled and taxes levied for their support, years before the act finally became a law.

Several questions suggest themselves in regard to the act of 1702, one of which is, who were the persons on whom the poll tax was levied? A law passed in 1715 gives us the enumeration, the same providing for the duties of the constable in making up the list under the law: All males and all female slaves above the age of sixteen years. An act of 1662, had fixed the age for slaves at ten years. Also by a law of 1725 all female mulattoes born of white women, and all free negro women were taxables; the only exceptions being beneficed clergy, paupers and aged slaves. For from the foundation of Maryland the negroes had been found in the colony, one having landed in Maryland with the first settlers. Found also to be profitable in working the lands they soon increased in numbers. They early became, however, a great subject of agitation, and continued to be until the institution of slavery ceased. Their great numbers were forced upon the colonies by the cupidity of the English merchants and government. The first matter however, about which difficulty arose with them, was not civil but religious. For it was argued by some that baptism was not possible for them, such being the position taken by some Quakers, as mentioned by the celebrated Thomas Story who was present at a meeting at West River, in the year 1699; the argument being that as the baptized are made in the rite "members of Christ, children of God and inheritors of the kingdom of Heaven" they could not any longer be detained as slaves; not that their care was in this for the slaves, which they themselves possessed for many years after this time, but they rejected the baptism. This is the same question, it will be remembered, St. Paul had to deal with.

In consequence of such notions, in some instances the negroes were sadly neglected, neither baptism administered nor instruction given, though the church labored hard, as the Maryland records show, through a long period to correct such false notions and to secure these blessings to the slaves. The state did the same by declaring the fallacy of the Friends' argument, enacting in 1715 the following: "For as much as many people have neglected to baptize their negroes or to suffer them to be baptized, on the vague apprehension that negroes by receiving the sacrament of baptism are manumitted or set free; be it hereby further declared and enacted that no negro or negroes by receiving the holy sacrament of baptism is thereby manumitted or set free, nor hath any right or title to manumission more than he or they had before; any law, usage, or custom to the contrary notwithstanding."

A second question in regard to the establishment is, what were the functions of the vestry under it? The vestry acted for the state in the erection and care of church buildings. For the churches were not built by private subscription, but in the beginning, and at any subsequent period when renewal might be necessary, money for the erection of churches and also for their repair, was levied upon the taxables of the parishes, either by the Assembly or the county court, as the case might be; while contracts were made by the vestry with power to draw on the sheriff for the amount assessed. They were also executive officers, in some respects, for the county court, selling immoral women and their children into slavery under the court's decree. It was their duty also to authorize the rector and wardens under an act of 1694 to publicly admonish persons living together immorally, a form of vice terribly prevalent at that time; for there were ten separate cases where parties were publicly admonished for this crime in August 1698 in St. James' Parish alone. The vestry also were preservers of the peace within the limits of the Church and Church yard, in some cases passing regulations directing the acts of the wardens. Afterwards other functions were added more truly secular, as the choosing of counters to prevent the excessive production of tobacco, the law limiting the amount that might be planted to every workman on the place. They also later down in the colony nominated inspectors of tobacco for the warehouses within their parishes; and at one period we find them returning officers for reporting persons liable to be taxed as bachelors to meet the expense incurred in the French war.

Their powers were, however, limited as compared with those of the vestries of Virginia. For to these was reserved such influence as to promote great confusion; while in Maryland the authority of the vestries was so contracted as that clerical licence was often exaggerated, producing jealousy and contention between pastor and people. For the seeing or imagining evils which they were unable to correct, only irritated the laity and widened immeasurably the distance between pastor and people. For in Maryland the vestry had no power but to receive the governor's or his Lordship's appointment of a rector, and when he was settled there was no legal authority in existence to remove him, though we find the commissary, Mr. Henderson, attempting to discipline certain derelict men. All power of presentation and induction was reserved, both by the charter and the act of 1702, to the civil authority, a fact that often excited extreme indignation on the part of the vestries, but a fact also that had to be endured; for the Proprietary prized all his prerogatives too highly to let one of them ever slip from him. Possibly under all the circumstances it was the best thing that could have happened; for under the restrictions Maryland was saved from many things that befell the church in Virginia, chiefly the last bitter experience of the latter when the Revolutionary struggle put an end to both establishments. The vestries, however, in Maryland wielded a very decided indirect influence, and when their opinions were strongly expressed, they were considered, as well by the governor of the province as by the legislators; and under the stimulus afforded by them the latter tried to prevent current evils, especially in the clergy; for repeated efforts were made by the Assembly to discipline offenders. Also, when the vestrymen themselves were men of character, which often they were not, they could hold evil doers in check. All general laws, however, proposed for disciplining the clergy proved abortive, even the best of the clergy, who often grieved over their offending brethren, resisting the means proposed as not in keeping with their conceptions of the independent position of ordained men, the attempt always being to create a court for trial composed in part of laymen.

As it will appear the position of a vestryman under the Establishment was different from what it is now. He was a man clothed with functions and dignities which are not now recognized as belonging to him. His eye was supposed to be everywhere, discerning wrong doing to correct it, and so he was the custodian of the morals and good order of society; and this he did, not as a grand juror will do now, but his functions were connected with the house of God, which was supposed, under the law, to embrace under its care all the citizens of the province, and so he was custodian of morals as in the sight of God. He may not always have recognized that fact himself, but the Establishment was only a less pronounced expression of that identity of church and state that prevailed in New England. The meeting of the vestry and wardens monthly was the convening of a spiritual court with a good many secular functions, and their separation from the rest of the congregation on Sunday as they gathered into their peculiar pews, whence they issued only to repress some irregularity, kept up the same conception. In conformity with this was a law of 1723, which forbade swearing or drunkenness in the presence of a vestryman, a church warden, and other persons named, under the penalty of fine, whipping, or sitting in the stocks ("a freeholder or other reputable person" being excepted from the latter form of punishment.)

In addition to these duties of the vestry, the chief vestryman, or minister, had other functions. One of these was the granting of marriage licences, which was appointed to him by Gov. Nicholson's proclamation in 1698. For Maryland has always thought it right to raise a revenue by this means, often in this way putting a bar in the path to matrimony. The aberrations, however, of legislators are sometimes striking; for while Maryland has always insisted on a fee for marrying, when she got very much pressed for funds in 1755, she immediately demanded of a man a fee for not getting married, and for years taxed the bachelor as such. Her chief desire evidently has always been not the man's happiness but his money. Another function of the chief vestryman was the reading of certain penal laws four times a year publicly, such laws being those concerning swearing, drunkenness, and the violation of the Sabbath day by work, fishing, gunning; and if he refused or failed to do this he was fined. For the statute books of Maryland have always been marked for liquor and Sunday laws, and the requirement of the Rector of the parish to read these publicly, shows what the Church was, the minister of the state for the working out of its own best condition. We have seen also what the duties of the minister and vestry were in regard to the immoral, whether married or unmarried, in the way of rebuke and punishment.

Altogether the impression left on the mind after reviewing the whole matter, is that while as an establishment, the church had many things to endure, which afflicted her intensely, for she was often wounded in the house of her friends; yet that she was of immense benefit to the then state of society in the colony, that she was a necessity for the elevation of the tone and character of the people, that there was no system that could have taken her place, that she wrought great good for the permanent welfare of Maryland, and that Marylanders perceived this; so that though they might be at times spiteful and disposed to strike heavy blows, yet that they instinctively recognized her merits and her good ends achieved, and preserved her integrity to the very last.

CHAPTER III.

THE POPULATION OF THE COLONY.

Before entering upon the closer work of our narrative it will be advisable to take a glance at the general make up of the population of the province, for the reason that the origin and elements of the population must have had a very strong influence at times, if not all along, upon the experience of the Establishment. For it was then in the colony, as it is now in England where the Non-conformists are so antagonistic to the church. The Establishment was always an occasion of wrangling, frequently excessive, both in the legislative halls and also in private, at times the question rising to the prominence of a great political agitation. The fact, however, that the Establishment continued to exist down to the Revolution proved that the great majority of the people were its favorers and supporters. For other great friends it had none, but was rather abused and oppressed and feared by those in power; and yet though the law, as providing for its emoluments was repeatedly altered, no hand was ever laid upon its life. Attempts were made by indirect means to annul the Establishment, as by declaring that the law had never been duly enacted. But these were probably only to feel the general pulse and the investigation told politicians it was a dangerous project.

Lord Baltimore's colony as first sent out, consisted of about two hundred, though one authority says three hundred persons. Among these there were about twenty gentlemen of "good fashion." These were probably all of either Great Britain or Ireland. At the same time there was a settlement upon Kent Island, of persons from Virginia, whose number was about one hundred. This was the population at the founding of the colony. There were settlements also on the Delaware founded by the Dutch; but as this territory, though originally included in the terms of Lord Baltimore's grant, was afterwards conferred upon another, we need not keep it in mind.

It is interesting also to observe the sources from which settlers afterwards came. For Maryland gathered within its borders persons from not only Great Britain and Ireland, but also from the continent, as France, Holland, Bohemia, Germany and Spain. The policy on which Lord Baltimore acted from the beginning, was in the highest degree judicious and enterprising. His aim and endeavor were to fill his territory in the quickest possible way. This was different from the plan that controlled some of the earlier settlements, for they were established as asylums from religious persecution, while Maryland was established, as some of the later colonies, as a business enterprise. Cecilius, Lord Baltimore, by whom the colony was finally

sent out, remained himself in England. He
regarded it, however, as a safe investment,
and spent large sums upon it. He also put
forth efforts to send out settlers, as his advertisement, already referred to, shows, while
Alsop's "Character of the Province of Maryland"
written in 1666 is believed to have been
prompted by the same cause. We know also
in other ways that Lord Baltimore labored hard
to this same end, soliciting and entering into contract with parties to bring settlers in. For this
reason he pursued the liberal policy he did,
though certainly his religious views compelled
him to the same; for a bigoted policy on his
part would not have been tolerated in the British
Empire for one day. It was doubtless also a
policy harmonious with his own enlightened
understanding; for there is nothing either in his
words or actions that can make us doubt that.
He invited all to come. He gave all a share in
the administration of the colony by giving them
a seat in the provincial assembly. He natural-
ized those who were of foreign extraction, and
while allowing religious liberty to all of whatever name, he was content to secure by law the
rights and liberties of those of his own faith.
And so the emigrants gathered in from all
quarters. It was the day of emigration. The
Old World was too small and too full. The
franchises of men were too contracted. The
oppressed Romanist of Britain yearned for religious freedom, and the oppressed Protestant,
whose religion had developed within him a
desire for broader privileges, sought deliverance
from the surviving remains of feudalism whose

spirit was antagonistic to all political right. Privilege and prerogative, the one the possession of the higher classes, and the other in scanty measure, the gift to all others, were at the foundation of the old world's legislation. The new world's open doors were hailed as the great refuge. God's intention in this last discovery was perceived. Maryland, in her earlier days offering a freer asylum than most of the other colonies did, received her full share of those who were looking for such a refuge. Besides, as the founder's terms were very liberal, the poverty stricken at home could with confidence look forward to competence within his domain; while also it was easy for any one that desired it to secure a passage out by obligating himself to labor for a certain period when he reached his destination.

But it was not only the voluntary emigrants that came into the colony. There were others, as the Scotch prisoners, who, having taken up arms or shown sympathy for the Pretender in 1715 or 1745 were sent out of the country. There was also another kind of emigrant, of a far more objectionable type, the convicts, persons found guilty of various felonies. According to one authority, quoted by McMahon, for thirty years, ending in 1767, the average number of this class received into the colony and purchased by the colonists for their labor, had been six hundred. This was a kind of emigrant that the residents of the colony of Maryland, as the residents in every other colony, were most unwilling to accept, as it was a gross injustice to precipitate such a class in such numbers upon

them. It was, however, very convenient for
the government at home. Still another body
of the population was the negroes who had
grown to the number of 49,675 in the year 1761.
This was not by natural increase of course.
The slave trade had been fondly nurtured by
the English government as one of its dearest
possessions, and the provinces also had looked
upon it with favor, as affording them a cheap
and efficient supply of labor. All the colonies
of America rejoiced in the opportunity, except
as the cupidity of the English merchants forced
upon the market an excessive supply. Kidnapping of grown persons and children was also
extensively pursued in Great Britain and Ireland
to supply the colonial demand.

This was, therefore, the population of Maryland.—of various, and it might seem, of heteroge-
neous elements. Except, however, in the case of
the negroes, the whole body, convicts, prisoners
of war, foreigners of all classes, English, Irish,
Scotch, and from the continental nations became
amalgamated into a homogeneous body, and at
the close of the colonial period the whole people
were found united in one aim and kindled with
one desire. We would not of course expect to
find the social condition of a people so constituted very high. There were wealthy men and
men of culture all the way through the whole
colonial period, but also the larger body of the
inhabitants must have been ignorant and of a low
moral standard. We shall see evidences of this
latter condition as we go on; while the absence
of any provision for instruction in the beginning
and the scanty supply throughout the whole

time, make the former certain. The early want, too, of church ministrations, from the great scarcity of Christian ministers, helped to keep the moral and intellectual tone low. For the sparse settlement of the territory made cooperation for clerical support almost impossible, even if the people themselves had had any longing for such ministrations; and the colonial authorities did not feel themselves under obligation to make provision in the case. There were some ministers, but very few. After the establishment of the church and of the Royal authority in the colony, religion and education both were provided for, with an attempt to make the provision sufficient. The Establishment so far wrought great good, and in the only possible way, at this time. The opening of a future, however, to all the settlers who might have an ambition to improve their condition, was itself a great educational influence, with the result of developing a tone and character in the population superior to that found in like classes in the home country. This sense of a future has always been to the American masses the profoundest cause of their social elevation

The make up of the colonists in the matter of their religious sentiments, presents as great a diversity as the places of their nativity or the reasons for their coming into the province. As we have seen, the evidence is unquestionable that the great majority of the first colonists were of the Protestant faith. "In leading the colony to Maryland by far the greater part were heretics," says the Jesuit Father; and the assembly that met in 1638 was "composed with few exceptions of heretics," an assembly, it will be recollected, where all freeholders were present either personally or by proxy. This throws light upon the ordinance of the following year which secured to "Holy Church" her rights, and which, as now understood meant only to secure the church against exactions of the temporal power. From the beginning these two classes were found in the colony. And Alsop, writing in 1666, indentifies the heretics, calling them by the now much abused title "Protestant Episcopal," equivalent to Protestant Catholic used in the colony in 1642. "With few exceptions the colony was composed of heretics" so the Jesuit father. In 1681, there were thirty Protestants to one Papist, according to Chalmers; while in 1700, according to Dr. Bray, the Roman Catholics numbered one twelfth, the same ratio that is given for the year 1754.

The Protestants, however, presented a solid front only to the Roman Catholics. They were greatly divided among themselves, Maryland being by its liberal government a haven of rest to many that were persecuted and driven out from the other provinces as well as from the countries beyond the sea. Among the first of such persons to come in were the Puritans, who, having been ordered to leave Virginia where they had been settled for some years, took up their residence at the mouth of the Severn. Virginia and Massachusetts were at this time acting as twin sisters in repression, only with contradictory antagonisms, Virginia abominating the Puritans as much as Massachusetts abominated all those who in any way disagreed with its own church principles. It was the time when

Puritanism was triumphant in England, when Presbyterianism followed the Anglican church in being driven from authority, when Independency was supreme. Virginia had not hesitated on this account, but compelled the withdrawal of the co religionists of Cromwell and his army. They entered the province in the year 1649, and for some years took an active part in and fomented the disturbances of the period, defying the authority of Lord Baltimore and refusing to take the oaths which had been imposed as a condition of plantation. Afterwards they quieted down, and probably in the great changes which took place in that part of the colony when the capital was removed thither, became absorbed in large measure in the church.

Another class that entered the colony in its earlier days were the Quakers, whose presence is first determined in the year 1657. The first appearance, however, was of persons rather bent on missionary enterprise, travelling members acting in that proselyting spirit that has always more or less distinguished their society until more recent years. Nor were their endeavors without success; for we see that they were soon able to establish their meetings on both shores of the Chesapeake. In 1672 George Fox, the founder of the sect, attended a meeting at West River which he describes as large and which lasted four days. Members of course came in from abroad as new colonists, to a place where unusual consideration was shown them; but many converts were made in Maryland; one reason for which probably was the fact above noted, the difficulty the settlers had in a sparsely settled country to provide by voluntary contributions for the support of ministers. Often for long periods there were no opportunities offered for public worship, a blessing very many of the people yearned for, and the opening of a Friend's meeting was the best possible provision under the circumstances. The children were not baptized, holy communion was not administsred, the Word was not preached. Quakerism came in with its negations in regard to this whole work of the ministry, and, a new thing, it commanded a large amount of attention. Besides, those who represented the new sect must have been men of force who would constrain attention. Certainly they were very sincere and devotedly in earnest. They were willing and did endure all things. Many of them suffered even unto death, though not in Maryland. Here some attempts were made to repress them, but they soon got influence and as early as 1677 some of them appear to have been members of the Assembly. They largely, also, increased in numbers, so that in the year 1700, when the population of the colony was probably twenty-five thousand, they numbered about one-twelfth. In subsequent days the law took pains to protect them, as from the presence of disorderly men at their yearly meetings, while already such adaptation of the laws as was necessary in what they esteemed matters of moment, as keeping the head covered, or affirming instead of swearing in the courts, had been made.

It is a notable thing, however, in Maryland history that where at one time the Quakers abounded and had flourishing meetings, now they are not found at all. This is the fact in various places, but West River presents a very marked instance. Here the old burying ground is found, and here are the families whose names adorn the old records, but there is not a Friend anywhere in the whole region. Farther up the country there is an old meeting house standing, but only as a deserted relic of the past; and farther down the country the site is pointed out of another house. The cause of the disappearance of the membership is to be found, of course, in some social change that has affected the body in times gone by ; for in other regions the disciples of Fox have shown sufficient tenacity of life. The great Hicksite-schism may have unhinged the views of some ; but the great probable cause that undermined this ecclesiastical fabric was the antagonism to slavery, which became in the last half of the eighteenth century so strong a sentiment with the Friends, that to hold slaves debarred persons from continuing members of the society. This final resolution we are told, encountered serious opposition from many members, most probably those who lived in that section of the country where slavery continued to be the chief dependence for labor ; and consequently the question being presented of abandoning their farms or abandoning their meeting, many were found who could not see the heinousness of the ancient institution which even the Quaker principles had always allowed to this time. And so it was as the years passed on they lost their former reverence for the peculiarities of their persuasion, and by degrees conformed to the doctrines and practices of the people among whom they lived. This is the most probable conjecture, and is fortified by still existing tradition.

Another sect that settled in Maryland about the year 1680, was a company of Labadists, a body that lived on communal principles. They were few in number, and were in various ways attractive, but though ambitious of proselytes, they gained but few. Their existence, however, was short-lived in Maryland. They came from Friesland, founded by Labadie, formerly a priest of the Roman Communion, a Frenchman who settled in Holland. Their views and practices were in many ways peculiar.

Of course there were in addition to these all the various forms of dissent from the Established church. For toleration, though for a short while in a measure denied, soon was allowed most fully, the Roman Catholics, also, having all religious privileges, though denied equal political rights. These other sects, however, did not come in with demonstration, but were content to enjoy and rejoice in the liberty which in some cases they were denied at home. The Scotch brought over their Presbyterian affiliations, the Germans their Lutheran organization, while from incidental remarks we know that in the earlier period, and probably all the way along, there were Jews as well as other unbelievers in the province. The composite character of the religious proclivities of the people was brought out in the year 1760, when Boston having suffered very greatly by fire, the Governor of Maryland called on the citizens of the province to contribute for the relief of the sufferers. The response was liberal, one thousand, eight hundred and thirty-nine pounds, given approximately as follows: by the Established Church, fifteen hundred and three pounds, by the Quakers one hundred and thirty-four pounds, by the Presbyterians one hundred and seven, by the Roman Catholics seventy-six, by the Baptists seven, by the Dunkers six, by the Lutherans five. These items are interesting as showing not only the religious denominations within the province, but also in some degree they may be supposed to indicate their relative numbers. Doing so, they show, also, why the establishment continued to be, notwithstanding a large amount of wrangling and dispute from time to time, an accepted institution to the close of the colonial days. It contained within it the great body of the people, and it embraced the great influential class that by its intelligence swayed the legislature and by its wealth supported the government. It takes but a few men to begin an agitation and those few may be controlled by unworthy reasons, which they may be loth to make known to the world. An institution is fixed in a community because it rests upon the fixed sentiment of the great mass of the people and presents to their heart and mind strong reasons for its existence. Nothing else than this can account for the solidity of the establishment amidst all kinds of agitation that raged around it and in it through the whole period of its existence and the gracious farewell that was extended to it at last, and the quasi recognition of its principle that was contained in the Bible of Rights. The establishment was always supported by the best sentiment and willingly sustained by the preponderirg wealth of the people.

CHAPTER IV.

THE CARRYING OUT OF THE ACT OF ESTABLISHMENT.

The Act of Establishment though passed in May 1692 was not carried out till January 1694 or rather 1695, according to our present division of the year, and that for the reason, apparently, that Gov. Copley, who was the first governor of the now Royal Province, did not feel any strong interest in the matter, with enough of other things during his brief administration, to engross his attention. He was succeeded by Gov. Nicholson, who reached the colony in 1694, and at once by his vigor the law was carried into effect, and the territory laid out into parishes. Gov. Nicholson was to the province of Maryland in the highest degree a blessing during the period of about four years which he continued in it. No man of that time, may be, has been more severely criticised by our historians than he, though often it would seem with a kind of mock liberality of political sentiment. In fact, frequently in reading their denunciations of the men and measures of those times there appears a want of true appreciation of the times in which the objects of their abomination lived and labored. There is no sense in judging a man of the seventeenth century by laws that have grown out of the advancement that has taken place since the seventeenth century. What would be an arbitrary measure now would not have been an arbitrary measure then. What would be a lofty and imperious manner now in the case of some public protest, in the midst of a people all of whose officers are of their own choosing, passing ministers of their will, would not have been a lofty and imperious manner in the days when kings ruled, and when the limits of constitutional authority were indefinitely understood both by kings and people. So, to read such strictures now, as we sometimes find our nineteenth century historians indulging in, rather palls upon the ear, and it becomes our desire to leave their judgments and ascertain their facts. Governor Nicholson seems to have been a man of hasty temper and impatient of restraint. He seems also to have had the unfortunate faculty of pursuing any object of his antipathy relentlessly. At the same time, while it is the fashion now to say hard things of him, very pleasant things were said of him while he was governor of Maryland, as the council proceedings show, things highly commendatory of his course; the final testimonial of this nature being given in 1698 when his authority in Maryland ceased. In Virginia, also, he was very popular, a handsome donation, as a testimonial, having been voted him, though it is true he was not there uninterruptedly popular. Years afterwards, also, when he became governor of South Carolina, he was held in high favor, and in such completed a long political association with the colonies.

This was the man that without any special appointment for this reason, became the patron of the cause of the Church in Maryland under the recently enacted law; and coming into power he immediately set about establishing the church's influence. Regarding the law as going into effect upon its passage, as it did, he caused the accumulated tax to be used in building churches, while also he had the gratification of being able to induct eight ministers into Cures. Some of these, it appears, had accompanied him to the colony. His influence, also, made the establishment very popular as far as his influence was needed; and we are informed "the churches were crowded as full as they could hold." This, as already surmised, was not only because the governor favored the church and clergy, but probably also because it was the first opportunity furnished for the general assembling of the people in protestant places of worship; and there was a strong yearning at that time to worship God under the ministrations of a protestant ministry. The antagonism of the whole protestant body to the Roman Church, with which sentiment the air was charged, both in England and America, made even dissenters glad to embrace the establishment as a strongly felt want. Probably never at any time, either in !England or in the colony, was there a nearer approach to an accommodation on the part of dissenters and churchmen than now. This had been brought about by the common uprising of all classes against the perfidious but plausible designs of James II. Both the Act of Toleration and the proposed Act of Comprehension testify to this. Gov. Nicholson did all he could to make the Church of England acceptable to the whole body of the people, and he so far succeeded as that opposition to it was not found among the non-conformists in general, but only among the widely separated bodies, the Quaker and Roman Catholics.

Another subject which early excited his interest was that of education. Before coming into Maryland, while Lieutenant Governor of Virginia, he had secured the establishment of the College of William and Mary, and while he did not attempt so elaborate an enterprise in Maryland his aim was to provide free schools throughout the province. In 1696 the attempt was repeated in an act petitioning the king for liberty to establish a school in every county. The idea was, that such schools should be feeders to William and Mary College. The attempt was in a measure successful and various schools were opened. It is highly probable that such a system was supplemented by parochial schools conducted by the clergy. There is frequent evidence of this given; though with both opportunities the standard of education in the province must have been low. There were always some men of high attainments, among them a small number who had been sent to Europe to complete thetr training. The mass of the people, however, had neither the appreciation nor the leisure to attain more than the rudiments.

Besides Governor Nicholson, Maryland was

also extremely fortunate at the same time in the possession of another eminent man in the administration of her affairs. This was the Rev. Dr. Bray who for some years acted as commissary, a church officer whose duty was to have supervision of the clergy and a certain oversight in the regulation of church matters. It is difficult to speak very clearly about his influence, because the office was at best but a passing adaption to a passing need. He possessed none of the powers of the episcopate. He was only the Bishop's representative for supervision to take cognizance of cases, to warn the unruly. In Dr. Bray's case the office was highly respected. Afterwards, however, when it came into other hands, and jealousies were excited, it is questionable whether often it did not do more harm than good. Pretensions were put forth on the one side and a grasping after authority, which were resisted with violence and virulence. Dr. Bray occupied a relatively higher position than any one that succeeded him did. He was in the colony but a short time. Efforts were often made by the clergy, sometimes jointly with the civil authority, to secure the residence of a Bishop. Even at this early date such an effort was made. The Bishop of London was ordinary for the colonies, though this title was sometimes given to the Governor of Maryland ; but of course the benefit of such an arrangement was small compared with the influence a Bishop on the spot might exercise. Discipline was always at fault, and incalculable harm was often done by unworthy ministers. Ordination to the holy ministry could only be obtained by crossing the sea, and so the supply was kept down. Dependence was altogether upon clergymen from Great Britain, many of whom left their country for their country's good. Confirmation of course could never be administered.

To obtain a Bishop, however, was impossible in the then state of things, and so as the next best thing a commissary was chosen and sent out. This was done at the solicitation of the clergy, who desired that the officer sent might be "capacitated to redress what is amiss and supply what is wanting in the church." There was no law of the colony providing for such an officer, neither had regulation been made for his support or for his authority over the person of the citizens, whether clerical or lay ; questions that were to excite in the coming days a great deal of discussion and bitterness. Dr. Bray was readily fixed upon for the office, having by his writings had the attention of Dr. Compton called to himself, and in 1696 he was chosen. He did not immediately, however, go over to his province, but remained in England till the close of 1699, reaching the colony early in the next year. It was the peculiarly good fortune of Maryland to have had at the same time two such ardent friends laboring for her, Governor Nicholson in immediate administration of her civil affairs and Dr. Bray using all his endeavors to forward her best religious interests. For the latter was indefatigable in his efforts to provide for his jurisdictions not only ministers to whom he offered many worthy inducements, but also parish libraries of the best works of the day for the information of the clergy, and through them of the people. He regarded this as one of the best things he could accomplish. For many of the clergy of the time, though duly ordained, were greatly wanting in training, so that a subsequent governor expressed his surprise how such unprepared men could ever have entered the ministry. The hope of a supply of ministers at all was, of course, chiefly from the poorer of the home clergy. Only such could in any numbers be expected to brave the difficulties of the long sea voyage with its attendant risks in those days, and to undergo the unknown trials of a colonial life. So he felt parish libraries to be a great necessity, and succeeded in establishing about thirty in Maryland, with others in other parts of America, as well as some also in England.

We at this day can hardly appreciate the need there was of such provision at that time. A home far away from the centre of publication, the price of books high, the salary of the clergy small as a rule, with nothing like our current literature, which whatever may be said of its value, at any rate gives the mind some exercise, an uneducated people whose demands upon the clergy were not stimulating, constituted a crowd of obstacles enough to reduce the standard of clerical attainment to the smallest. Dr. Bray endeavored in his capacity of commissary, to provide relief for this, and made personal solicitations to the wealthy. Where he found an unwillingness to contribute for the use of the colony he endeavored to secure something for feebler parishes at home. The libraries sent out differed very greatly in numbers, that of St. Ann's parish, Annapolis, having a thousand and ninety-five volumes. They were committed to the care of the rector, being intended for his use, who was bound to see that the books were preserved. Most of these collections have long since been scattered, but from time to time a separate book is picked up in some old parish. St. John's college, Annapolis, has quite a number of them in its keeping. The disorder into which everything fell during the Revolution and subsequently, was the cause of the loss. They would hardly, however, even if they were still in existence, possess more than an antiquarian interest.

Dr. Bray's efforts to secure clergy for the parishes, were so far successful that when he came into the colony he found, including such as came with him, seventeen. These all came expecting to be supported by the provision made for them in the province, that is, by the Act of Establishment. For though Missionaries were sent out by the great English Society for Propagating the gospel, to other parts of America, yet Maryland was supposed to be able to take care of itself. That Society was indeed the child of Dr. Bray's own heart and mind in a most eminent degree. Its field, however, was in other parts of America. Yet Maryland did not make any abundant provision. Each parish was to take care of its own rector, and consequently there was a great difference in the value of the livings. The supposition was that the average sum for a living would be about one hundred pounds sterling, but actually the income in some places was not more than a quarter of that. The chief cause of this difference was the varying character of the population, some sections of the colony being far more thickly settled than others. An attempt was made in the beginning to compensate for this by making the parishes in the thinly settled portions much larger, a means that later produced sometimes irritating and painful results, while in the beginning it made the labors of the rector often very excessive. The irritating circumstances arose from the fact that when the territory filled up, the incumbent had far more to do than he had time for, and the people were thus denied Church opportunities, and yet, as the incumbent's salary was contingent upon the number of polls, he was opposed to a division. Besides, inducted into the whole parish he regarded a division as an interference with his vested rights. The division, however, took place; though sometimes the difficulty was provided for by the erection of chapels of ease and the appointment of assistants. Another circumstance made the income to vary from year to year, the varying quality and market value of the currency in which all colonial officers were paid, tobacco. Attempts were made to fix a rate of commutation in the scrip of the colony, but the planters could always get the better of the parsons in that, by paying in what medium they pleased. Some of the parishes after a few years yielded very handsome incomes, while some others were always extremely weak.

The whole arrangement produced many difficulties throughout the whole colonial period. In some parishes the scantiness of the clergyman's income caused better men to make special provision for their support, and a number of cures early received endowments in land. Pluralities were allowed, as we have seen, under certain conditions, but the necessary labor involved often meant practical inefficiency. In some respects Maryland had a show of prosperity which was not always justified by the facts.

Dr. Bray, having come into the colony, immediately began the duties of his office. In the May following his arrival, having previously visited each parish, he called together the clergy at Annapolis, now for six years the capital of the colony, when a general discussion was had upon matters bearing upon the good of the church. The visitation lasted several days, and the best feeling prevailed. He exhorted the clergy to diligence in the instruction of the young, in parochial visiting, in Catechising in the church, and in private where great distances prevented families from attending service; to be earnest in teaching the duty of seeking baptism, of which there had been great neglect, the opportunities also in most places having been few; and to begin the regular monthly administration of the Holy Communion as soon as a sufficient number of persons could be found desirous of receiving the same. Great satisfaction was expressed at the recent passage of a new act of establishment, which had been by the unanimous consent of the Assembly; thanks were extended to Governor Blackiston for his support in the matter, and reference was made to the necessity of discipline for the clergy, looseness of morals on their part being declared the greatest obstacle that could afflict the colony. One minister was severely arraigned in the presence of his brethren, his conduct being seemingly most extreme, and a time was appointed for his trial; an assumption of authority on the commissary's part that was not accorded to his successors. A scheme was laid out for several visitations a year, one of them to be a general visitation annually, when all the clergy were to be convened. Before their final separation the clergy joined in a request to the commissary that he would return to England to further the cause of the establishment act passed this year, and also to secure, as far as possible, an increase in the number of ministers. One item among their proceedings is of peculiar interest. It was a contribution made by the clergy assembled for the support of a missionary among the Quakers of Pennsylvania. They are described as "sadly deluded into a total apostasy from the Christian faith," and the clergy, rejoicing in their own privilege, as a kind of thank offering determined to recover as many as possible from the error of their way. Pennsylvania was regarded probably as a field for foreign missions; for there were many Quakers in Maryland for whose conversion the clergy might have both labored and contributed. The Act of Establishment, however, had not put these latter in a proper frame of mind for conversion; while for some years Pennsylvania had been very greatly excited and divided by a violent religious discussion, in the midst of which a very considerable number of Quakers had repudiated their former views. This was therefore felt to be an opportunity. The amount subscribed was twenty-five pounds sterling, to be paid annually, and the commissary of Virginia was solicited to promote the same endeavor amongst his clergy. It was a decided advance upon the old way of treating the Friends, and indicates a degree of earnestness which we are sometimes disposed to think did not exist in those days. Many of the pastors who came over to Maryland at that time, were certainly men of Christian tone and devotion. Dr. Bray acceded to the request to return to England, and it was well for the Church that he did; for without his resolute endeavors the act of 1702 would never have been finally approved. He did not return to America, though until his death, some thirty years after this time, he continued the steadfast friend of the Church in Maryland. One cause probably of the cessation of his connection with the Establishment, was his disappointment about his support. For it was expected that as commissary he should be made judge in testamentary cases, an office which would have yielded him three hundred pounds sterling per annum. As it was it was denied him, and also again when he sought it in his successor's behalf; and the agitation of the subject produced only bitterness with the civil authority. For the commissary as such there was no provision made. Dr. Bray had been most liberal with his own funds while laboring for the colony, and his means were now greatly contracted.

As to the immediate influence of the new position of the church for good upon the moral condition of the colony, we are not left in darkness. The difference between a community ministered to by clergymen and one where the gospel is not preached, ought to be apparent. A new community without the gospel is, as we find it in our own day, a place where looseness abounds, and that such was the condition of things in Maryland before the year seventeen hundred there is sufficient testimony. Such a promiscuous gathering of men could not but be regardless of the proprieties of life, and the only thing that could save the Maryland manners, was the fact that there were no great communities of men, there being but very few places that had the name and much fewer that had the appearance of towns. The condition of things at the time of the Protestant Revolution, we have seen. Dr. Bray, however, was able to assure the clergy that he had learned, while going from parish to parish, that the effect of the clergy's presence, the preaching of the gospel, and the uprightness of life which they themselves exemplified in their various fields, had produced immediate good. Evil men proved a drawback from time to time, but many good men, some of them marked for their excellence, also abounded; and the people received a positive blessing, of which, after the first noted effects, they ceased to be sensible. It is by contrast alone we often get to know of the most important facts, and the immense good the Establishment was working all the time, the terrible depravity from which it was saving the colony, was never discerned. It was doubtless the bulwark of right living till its closing days, when the increase of population prepared the way for the introduction of the voluntary principle.

CHAPTER V.

THE ORGANIZATION OF THE PARISH.

We have now come to the organization of the parish and the incidents accompanying it. These present many odd features to our conception; though Maryland notions were probably not very different from those of the home country in regard to like things. First must be remembered that this was in the days when the alliance between the church and state was such, to the exclusion of higher thoughts in large measure, that the tone and feeling of the church were greatly secularized. Some of the purest and noblest men shone eminently in that period, with Tillotson, Archbishop of Canterbury at their head. The Church's true relation, however, to the spiritual welfare of the people, was often obscured, and place was too frequently the object which priests and spiritual rulers had in their minds. With this of course came about a low spiritual standard among the people. Yet the colonists of Maryland were not wanting in earnestness, though in some things they were wanting in refinement of perception, and things were imposed upon the clergy by law and methods pursued for the house of God that would to us seem impossible.

The parish of St. James, Herring Creek, was laid out in the year 1694 (O. S.) by certain councillors and justices, Anne Arundel County being divided into four parts. The record runs thus: "Att a court held att London Town ye 31st day of January anno Dom. 1694 and in ye sixth year of the reign of our Sovereign Lord and Lady Willm. and Mary by ye grace of God of England, Scotland, France, and Ireland King and Queen, Defender of ye faith &c. By ye justices and councillors thereunto authorized, with ye most principal freeholders and others called for ye laying out of ye county of Ann Arundel into districts and parishes, in pursuance to an Act of Assembly entitulled an act for ye service of Almighty God and ye Establishment of ye Protestant Religion in this province made att ye citty of St. Mary's the tenth day of May Anno Dom. 1692.

Councillors and Justices present

Coll Nicholas Greenbury } Councillors.
The Hon. Thos. Tench Esq. }

Mr. James Sanders,
Maj. Henry Ridgley,
Capt. Nich. Gasaway,
Mr. Henry Constable, } Justices.
Mr. Philip Howard,
Mr. John Dorsey,
Mr. Seth Biggs,

Whereas, in pursuance of ye authority to us given by ye afore mentioned act, it is found convenient and is hereupon concluded that this County of Ann Arundell be divided into four parishes, the bounds and limitts of St. James' parish, then called by ye name of Herring Creek parish in Herring Creeke hundred with ye residue of West River hundred beginning at ye Southmost bounds of South River parish on ye land of Ewen upon Ewenton, now in the possession of Richard Gallaway, and bounding on ye East with ye bay of Chessepeake lieing down Southerly to ye creek called Fishing Creek then West with ye said creek to ye bounds of Ann Arundel and Callvert Countys to Lyons Creek, then with ye said creek to Potuxan, then up ye sd river to ye land called Whites Plaines to the Southernmost bounds of South River parish. And from White's Plains Easterly including ye ——and plantation of Thomas Stockett, Coll. Thomas Taylor's quarter, and by his dwelling plantation,—by John Wooden, Richard Wigg, Seaborn Batty, Doctor Ferdinandoe Batty, and so to the aforementioned bounds of ye land called Ewen upon Ewenton."

The commission having so far concluded its labors, the next thing to do was the organization of the parish, which was done under an order of the commission to the sheriff requiring him to give notice "to ye freeholders to meet at ye place hereinafter mentioned on ye second Thursday in February next ensuing, and there make choise of six ye most able men to be a vestry for the parish as aforesayd, and that ye clerk issue out summonses to ye sheriff for that purpose, which was accordingly done. Att which day the freeholders of ye parish of Herring Creek and part of West River hundred (id est) St. James' parish at ye day and time aforesaid mett att ye house of John Willson Sen. in ye said parish and then and there did ellect and choose for their vestry, viz:

Hon. Thos. Tench Esq., Mr. James Rigbie,
Mr. Seth Biggs, Mr. Nicholas Turrett,
Capt. Wm. Holland, Capt. Robert Lockwood.

The parish was thus organized, and in the following April the vestry elected the Church wardens, Mr. Wm. Holland and Mr. Abraham Brickhead, to serve for the ensuing year. Their first care was to qualify themselves for their office, and to do so they provided themselves with a copy of the law under which they were acting; according to which, there were various oaths appointed by act of Parliament which they were compelled to take. This was not done till the following August. The oaths were eminently ironclad, and covered grounds which to our minds lie outside ecclesiastical relations, properly so called. The only thing that can be said is they were in harmony with the then institutions. They were as follows:

First, I do sincerely promise and swear that I will be faithful and bear true allegiance to his Majesty King William. *So help me God.*

Second, I do swear that I do from my heart abhor, detest and abjure, as impious and heretical the damnable doctrine and position that princes excommunicated or deprived by the Pope or any authority of the see of Rome, may be deposed or murthered by their subjects or any other whatsoever.

Third, and I do declare that no foreign prince, person, or prelate, or potentate, hath or ought to have any jurisdiction, power, superiority, prominency, or authority, ecclesiastical or spiritual within the realm of England or the dominions thereunto belonging. So help me, &c.

There was also this test required of every church officer: We the subscribers do declare that we do believe that there is not any transubstantiation in ye sacrament of the Lord's supper or in the elements of bread and wine at or after the consecration thereof by any person or persons whatsoever.

Also the following injunction was required to be given: You shall well and truly act and do— in every station,—without prejudice, favor or affection, with equal rights to all persons, and shall not diminish or detain from any minister legally qualified and presented, inducted or appoynted by his excellency or other ways, any right, perquisite or benefit given by law. So help you God.

These oaths reflect the fears and jealousies of the times, and grew out of that period when the Church of England was so greatly endangered, as well also as the liberty of the people, in the last days of Charles II, and more notably in the time of James II, whose acts looked to the building up of an absolute government in England and the establishment of the church of Rome, to which both of them had conformed.

It was also an old claim of the Roman see that the Pope had power to absolve subjects from their allegiance, thereby inciting fanatics to murder their rulers; a claim that had more than once been acted upon in England. The matter also at this time assumed very imposing proportions when the fugitive King James was plotting his restoration, and was in correspondence with many in England who were watching by any available means to secure his restoration and thus undo the work of the Revolution; a danger that threatened England for more than a half century. The whole empire was, therefore, exceedingly jealous, and care was taken by every means to provide against disloyal men getting an opportunity of doing harm. This was in a large measure the cause of the laying of restrictions upon Roman Catholics everywhere in the British Empire. The immense presumption of that church excited suspicion against its members.

The parish thus established was one of thirty into which the province was divided. This division affords quite a fair opportunity for our seeing how the settlements were then distributed, being nearly all adjacent to the water courses; and the subsequent reports made from time to time of the condition of the parishes and number of families, show the relative strength of the population in the different sections. Much of the colony was not occupied at all in 1695, while the immense size of many of the parishes shows that the population in them was exceedingly scanty. For one reason of their great extent was that persons enough might be included to provide for the minister of the cure a competence; though often they failed to do this, as in some instances the income was not more than twenty-five or thirty pounds. What we call Western Maryland was then hardly known at all,

Prince George's County being without western limits. As the population increased new counties were set up, and also new parishes were created.

When the vestry assumed charge of the parish they found an old church already existing, the church of the original Herring Creek Parish; and curiously enough its name has passed over into popular use to the present parish. This older edifice is supposed to have been situated near the present village of Friendship, in the same neighborhood with the Quaker meeting house whose site is still pointed out. This is likely, as Herring Creek was a local designation covering that territory and was the name also of the meeting house. It is probable that that was an earlier center to a considerable population than a more northern point; the settlements having apparently generally extended up the bay from the original capital of the colony; though it is true, the mouth of the Severn and the parts adjacent down as far as the South River district, had been settled long before this; chiefly, however, by Puritans. Beside this again, there had been in previous years several clergymen in Calvert county, who could and doubtless did supply this church. One of them was the Rev. John Yeo, who was in Calvert county in 1680. Another was the Rev. Paul Bertrand, who was sent out from England about 1685 by the king in response to the petition of Mary Taney. He had died in the colony.

When the old church had been built it is not possible to say, nor by whom. Previous to this time there had been no public provision made for building churches or supporting ministers; though efforts were made in 1676 to induce the proprietary to make such provision. His reply was that the four protestant ministers in the colony had each a plantation by which he could subsist. Such churches, therefore, as were built and kept open had to be provided by private subscription. That the old church had been built many years before is evident from the fact that in 1695 it had to be covered anew and eight hundred pounds of tobacco were ordered for the work. For some reason, however, either because it was not near enough to the center of the parish, or because it was not sufficiently large, aided by the fact that the means for building were plentiful, the vestry immediately set about building a new edifice, the contract for which was given out in 1695. The means were at hand, because it was provided for in the act of establishment that the tax for the support of the church should be levied from year to year; and when there was no incumbent in a parish the proceeds of the tax were to go to the repairing and building of churches. St. James' and most of the other parishes were in this way provided with means for this demand, and worthy buildings were erected; for when the law went into effect there were only three clergymen in the colony and in the year 1700 there were only seventeen, some of them having just come over. Funds therefore rapidly accumulated.

The new church was not very pretentious. We have the following description of it given, a fair type doubtless of most of them in Maryland: It was forty feet long, twenty feet wide and twelve feet high in the side walls, with seven window frames and arched roof. It was to be finished inside with "chancell and table, with rayl and banisters, pulpit, reading desk and clerke's seat, the church to be seeled from top to bottom with half inch plank, batined in pannells, pues to be built on each side of the church, shutters to every window, the porch to be seeled after the same manner." The door was on the South side, with a porch nine feet square before it. The description of this porch as given is: "Ye door archt, with railes and banisters on each side, ye roof to be shingled as ye church." The capacity of such a building according to our present arrangement of seats would be about one hundred and fifty sittings, though with the old style of square pews economy of space was not so much considered. As first built, however, it was sufficient for their needs, though as time went on it was in various ways enlarged and additional capacity provided. This was done either by increasing the length of the building or by the erection of galleries, or by taking into use a vestry house as an annex. These changes began as early as 1704, and were made with consent of the vestry by private individuals who obtained exclusive title to the pews so provided, with the right of alienating them. The number of taxables nearly doubled in the first twenty-five years of the parish history.

The church was a long while in finishing, various causes of delay having arisen. Also having already a place of worship there was probably not so much urgency, and though money was sure to come in it would require several years in which to accumulate a sufficient amount. Besides, though it is said that in some parts of Maryland the churches were without floors save what mother earth provided, certainly that was not the case here. If it was anywhere the fact it is a high testimony to the faithfulness of the people who would not wait to have the floors laid to commence their offering of worship, for the Assembly provided the means which was sure to be furnished in a short time. That there was such urgency throughout the colony for the beginning of holy worship there can be no doubt. The opportunity for prayer and praise was not given before there was a demand for it.

The work on St. James,' however, was not rudely or hastily done. For the "gentlemen" who had composed a large part of the original colony, never died out in Maryland; but all the way through the colonial days we find the evidence of their intelligence and force of character, not only in civil but also in social affairs; a condition of society which West River, with its rich and productive soil, was always able to cherish. This was the case at this time, so that we find every care which pride and love could bestow, manifested for the church and its appointments; and though small in size and plain according to our present tastes, it began at once to be and ever continued the center of the dearest and holiest associations. Later down in the century a change took place, and much taste and art were shown in the building and adornment, not only of churches and other public buildings, but also of private residences. In Annapolis and the adjacent country especially, are such examples presented, the architecture and elaborate workmanship often putting to the blush many of the pretentious efforts of this present time. Many honorable mechanics doubtless came to America, as to a new field which with its increasing wealth offered large opportunity to their genius and ambition; while beside there were many who came over involuntarily, men who, of practical skill in the mechanical arts, were for some delinquency or crime, transported from their homes to these shores. Tradition ascribes more than one elegant piece of adornment to this class. There was employed in the building of the first church of the parish one such involuntary immigrant whose time was bought by the vestry.

From the year 1695 till 1698 there was no settled rector in the parish; but the law had provided for that case by making provision for lay readers, so that we find one such reading the service regularly at two hundred pounds of tobacco a month. We find also a person who wandered about America very considerably, the Rev. Hugh Jones, preaching three sermons in the parish; for which he received four hundred pounds of tobacco. He appears a little later as the rector of Christ Church, Calvert co.; a man who was apparently fond of his pen and used it sometimes skillfully in depicting to the English imagination scenes that had entertained him here.

In the matter of providing for the church building in those days, there seems to have been some confusion as to the means. We have seen that one of the functions of the vestry was to sell, for a term of years, white women guilty of having mulatto children, a crime that in the early days of the colony was very frequently committed, showing the presence of a fearfully debased class of society. Such cases were tried before the county court, the vestries only executing the sentence. Nor was the evil soon abated, for in 1715 we find it re-enacted, with the same penalty of seven years servitude inflicted on the father, if a free negro. A white man also was similarly punished who should be the father of a mulatto, so strenuously did they labor against miscegenation; while so radical was the evil that the law was re-enacted in 1717 and 1728. But the strangest part was that such children were supposed to belong to the church, and the pecuniary profits resulting from the crime in the sale both of parents and children, went to the use of the church, though afterwards it was claimed by one of the best ministers ever in the colony, that such persons belonged of right to the clergy, a claim that was apparently recognized.

As at this time there was no rector in the parish we find the vestry using their opportunity and providing out of the thirty-two pounds sterling they had received from the sale of such persons, the following articles along with others. Their order was that the money be laid out in iron work, glass and other necessary things; but when the account was returned it was found to include in "necessary things" a surplice, with a "flagon, two cupps, one challice, and one fine mettle bason," for baptisms, as afterwards noted; a rather incongruous association one would think between the means and the end. The same bill of items enables us to get a

little nearer glance at the old church and the
people's estimate of comeliness; for we find five
pounds sterling paid for five yards of fine green
broadcloth, with three pounds for silk fringe and
fourteen shillings for four tassels. For embroidering the cloth, which was to be used for a pulpit
cushion, thirty shillings were paid; while for
fine down to be used in stuffing the same eleven
shillings were given, the whole being made up,
along with the carpet, for ten shillings. Truly
they had some regard for what was comely and
beautiful; while also they soon outgrew the
anomaly of holy vessels being purchased in the
way their pewter service was. For in 1701 we
find this entry: "The vestry of this parish,
taking into their serious consideration with what
decorous and good order ye Blessed Sacrament
of the Lord's supper is administered both in
their native country and other parts of this
province, and out of a pious and godly desire to
follow ye good example of their fellow christians
and brethren of the church of England, and in
obedience to a canon of ye same church; have
unanimously voted ye buying of plate to be
used at ye offertory and celebration of ye same
sacrament, and for ye purchase thereof subscribed
ye severall sumes following: Coll Wm. Holland
four pounds, Mr. Henry Hall three pounds, Mr.
Anthony Smyth three pounds, Mr. Chris. Vernon
three pounds, Mr. Seth Biggs four pounds, Capt.
Robt. Lockwood three pounds, Mr. Abraham
Brickhead three pounds, Mathias Clark one
pound, Morgan Jones one pound." To this we
find added: "His Excellency Governor Blackston
five pounds, Mr. Hen. Robison two pounds, Mr.

Rich. Harwood two pounds;" a total of thirty-four pounds sterling. The plate at this time obtained by the fruits of this "pious and godly desire," is, with the loss of one piece, still in use in the parish. As we shall see, other pieces of valuable plate came to the parish by private gift within a few years from this time and are still retained. The old pewter service soon ceased to be mentioned in any inventory given.

Among the items in the account above mentioned is one for nine locks for pews. This seems like an anomaly. For the church was built and afterwards was sustained, by a general tax laid upon all except those incapable of labor; the vestry in one instance having the power to make the assessment. The church would therefore apparently belong to all equally without any reserved rights, a free church in its most perfect manifestation. On the other hand the contrary was the fact to the degree that later down in the history we find it a misdemeanor, with the penalty of corporal infliction attached, for persons to "intrude" in others' pews. The pew doors were locked, and as it was the time of the old high back institution, there was probably not much intrusion done. The pews, it would seem, were regarded as the private possessions only of a few of the wealthier planters. Pews added at private cost might well be regarded as the private possession of those who were at the whole expense, as was sometimes the case. A free gallery also was an idea embodied in the plans for the church; and the wardens and vestrymen had their official seats to which strangers, especially distinguished ones, would be invited. Even in the Quaker meeting, it is said, there were places allotted for the dignitaries of the colony when they might be willing to grace the assembly with their presence.

With all these allotments, however, the church was not at first too small for the public demands. Rather there was jealousy on the part of the the provincial authorities that the edifice was too large, and the vestry had to make their report that such was not the fact. The desire expressed was that the church should be considered as open to all, an order passed by the vestry in 1698 reading "that ye church wardens give notice to ye constables and other persons within this parish, (except Quakers) to come to church every Sabbath day," a rather uncertain action on their part; for if it was an invitation why did they not invite the Quakers, and why were the constables called into use? It sounds more like a dim echo of other days when church going was obligatory and they would constrain if they could. The Quakers were, it is to be remembered, a cherished class at this time, at any rate in the mind of William III, and so they were not to be offended even by a seeming invitation. There were also Roman Catholics, as well probably as Christians of other names, residing in the parish. They were all "invited." The Quakers, it is true, had then their own meeting houses, which the others had not; but this was not a sufficient reason; for two years after this the church made a subscription to support a missionary among them in Philadelphia. Possibly the Quakers in Maryland were regarded as hopelessly incorrigible and too hardened to come in. They were at any rate not antagonized by an invitation. How far the rest of the world heeded we are not told, only we know that soon the church had to be increased in size.

All this time the Governor and council kept a strict surveillance over the vestry's actions, making inquires as to the expenditure of moneys and requiring a copy of the record of their proceedings. The inference to be made, however, from the records, is that there was no occasion for fault; for down to the period to which we have come, and for a considerable time afterwards the whole tone of the administration was exceedingly worthy. Though acting under the law they evidently rejoiced in the law, and were thankful for the blessed opportunities that the law alone could at that time have provided, of worshiping God in His holy house under the guidance of a duly ordained minister. Everything was done decently and in order. Immorality for the first time found something like an effectual check; and domestic misery growing out of the conjugal infidelity, which so alarmingly prevailed, was in some measure removed, as its cause was rebuked and held up to indignation and scorn. In the establishment Maryland received, as the unanimous voice of its representatives again and again declared, what was in the highest degree necessary for its moral, social and religious welfare.

CHAPTER VI.

THE FIRST RECTORSHIP.

The rectorship of St. James' parish was first filled by a man in every way qualified to affect the parish permanently for good, the Rev. Henry Hall. He was inducted May 7th, 1698 by Gov. Francis Nicholson, and continued to direct the affairs of the parish till the year 1722, a period embracing many exciting episodes in Maryland church life, in which Mr. Hall bore a prominent part. The form of the induction was as follows, a form greatly changed in the later days of the colony: "Gentlemen, the bearer hereof is ye Rev. Mr. Henry Hall, who is sent by the Right Honorable and Right Reverend Father in God, Henry, Lord Bishop of London, in order to officiate as a clergyman of the Church of England in this his majestie's province. I do, therefore, in his majesties name, appoint the said Mr. Henry Hall to officiate as a clergyman of ye Church of England in St. James' parish in Ann Arrundel County.

Given under my hand and seale att ye port of Annapolis this seventh day of May in ye tenth yeare of ye reigne of our Sovereigne Lord, William ye third, by the grace of God of England,

Scotland, France and Ireland King, Defender of ye faith, Annoq. Dom. 1698.

To ye vestrymen of St. James' Parish in Ann Arrundel County.

This it will be observed, was entirely the work of the Governor, who, under the present law and condition of things, exercised the power of presenting and inducting The function had belonged to the Lord proprietor under his charter, though of course he had never exercised it; and by the Act of Establishment the right was conferred upon the Governor. Afterwards when the province was restored to Lord Baltimore, though for many years the governor continued to induct, under the Act, yet finally Lord Baltimore fell back upon his chartered privileges, and the act of induction ran in his own name and the party presented was of his own choice. This was in harmony with the custom of England at that time, and with the common rule now when patrons present absolutely to livings; though there has been much agitation for the purpose of modifying the law within the last few years, and of bestowing some right and influence upon the parishioners in the choice of their ministers, a concomitant of the general development of liberal views in English life. Political views in Maryland were always liberal, and consequently the same agitation took place here more than a hundred years ago.

For the system was found in Maryland, as it has been found everywhere else, liable to the greatest abuse, and was the occasion of great crying evils through the whole colonial period. For unworthy men, finding it to their advantage to leave the mother country, because either their moral or intellectual condition was so low, and hearing of the opportunities in Maryland where the demands on the part of the civil authorities were not so rigorous, were constantly coming over; and as for a long while the supply of clergy was never overfull, it was easy for them to secure positions, and to hold them for life if they would. For once settled, they were raised above the liability of prosecution; and necessarily almost, any evil tendency in them, the outcome of vice or ignorance, was only fostered. Many and bitter were the complaints on the part of the better class of the clergy, of the civil authorities, and of the vestries and people. It was an evil, for which, however, no correction could be found till the very last. The appointment of a commissary was tried; but as he could do no more than warn and rebuke, his influence was feeble. At times he did assume more, and by some his assumption was acquiesced in; but that was only passing, and the office died of inanition. He was the representative of the Bishop of London, who in spiritual matters was ordinary for the colonies as the civil authority, the Governor, was in temporal relations; and one of the plans proposed was that the commissary should take evidence and transmit the same to the Bishop for final action, as only a Bishop can degrade a minister. In that way the civil rights of a rector in his parish might be vacated. When, however, it was attempted by the Governor, in 1718, to obtain from the Assembly sufficient power for this procedure, the clergy endorsing the Governor's action, the whole was negatived by the non-action of the Assembly, their jealousy of such authority causing them to lay the matter over. For America was always afraid of entrusting either legislative or judicial functions to any authority in Great Britain. The clergy also themselves did not heartily approve this scheme, the office of commissary, as possessing only delegated authority, not commending itself to their judgement as one in which much authority might be reasonably lodged. In some instances, even as it was, it was found in use to create a good deal of trouble and confusion, Dr. Bray's difficulty in London with Gov. Seymour being exceedingly painful, and Mr. Henderson's in America with all parties being disastrous in the extreme. The liability to collision from the conflict of jurisdiction was very great, and even in the hands of a discreet person, who still cared for the honor of his office, conflict was unadvoidable. It was doubtless therefore the leading of a wise Providence that the jurisdiction of the commissary was not enlarged, and that the office finally ceased to be exercised.

Another plan proposed for abating the evil was the erection of an ecclesiastical court. This was attempted in 1708 by the Assembly during the administration of Gov. Seymour, a gentleman who though well spoken of for his management of the colony's affairs, was bitterly antagonistic to any administration over the church other than his own. This was shown in his aversion to the appointment of a commissary with authority when he was applied to by Dr. Bray. The support proposed for the commissary he utterly rejected, and expressed in no courtly language his aversion for the office. The court proposed by the Assembly was to consist of three clergymen, three laymen and the Governor; and was to have jurisdiction even to the limit of suspending ministers from their functions. The mention of such acourt shows the great need for some corrective discipline; but of course, the plan given excited the greatest opposition on the part of the clergy, it being clearly seen at the time and stated, that it ignored the first principle of Episcopacy. Protest was immediately entered with the Bishop of London. Governor Seymour, however, did not comfirm the law, on the ground that he had not received instructions from home in regard to the matter. Governor Hart afterwards was disposed, on his own motion, to examine into a case where complaint had been made by a vestry of their minister; but was deterred by the jealousy of the clergy against any infraction of the principles of their church government. Nor was the above the only occasion when the attempt was made to set up such a court, as we shall see further on, the attempt being resisted by the same objecttions.

Another plan suggested for the cure of the evil was the appointment of a Bishop for the colonies. Sometimes the petition was for a Bishop for Maryland, sometimes that the settlements in America should be provided with two Bishops, one for the Western Islands, the other for the mainland. Sometimes the plea was sent in for a suffragan Bishop, as the representative of the Bishop of London in this part of his jurisdiction. This desire was expressed, also, not only by the clergy, but also by the commissary, and at one time by the civil authority; for all agreed that the only feasible mode of improving the condition of things was the appointment of a Bishop. All such pleadings, however, were neglected. It was proposed that the colony should support the Bishop, as it supported all its clergy. For the clergy of Maryland received no aid from home. The provision for his support was to be obtained by granting him the fees of the office for the probate of wills, and by a plantation of fifteen hundred acres of land. This was the plan suggested in 1724. There was no favorable response, however, from the administrators of colonial affairs in England. At one time it was feared that the appointment of Bishops for America would tend to create a feeling of independence in the colonies; and therefore of course it was avoided. Later on, about the year 1760, when the scheme was further urged by the English Bishops, not for Maryland particularly, but for America, the matter received earnest consideration in the English Cabinet. But the difficulties were felt to be at the time insurmountable. In 1768 both Massachusetts and Virginia are found in their legislative assemblies reprobating the establishment of Episcopacy in the colonies, a harmony of opinion in widely divergent quarters that could not but make the English government halt in carrying out any such purpose. Eddis, also, writing from Maryland in the closing days of the colony, says: "The colonists were strongly prejudiced against the Episcopal order."

These were the various means proposed for disciplining the clergy and undoing the evil effects of the ignorance or indifference of the governors in inducting unworthy men. How weighty was the evil it is impossible to say; for in such matters there is always much exaggeration. We have in the year 1723 a picture of ten of the clergy of the time, which will throw some light upon the question as showing the prejudices at work affecting the judgment, and, may be, suggest the ratio of unworthy men to the respectable. It will be observed that political antagonism is strongly expressed, and when we go back to that period, and remember the spirit of faction, that slumbered, indeed, at times, but was nevertheless strong, resting on the claims of the pretender as against the reigning house of Hanover, and also the ecclesiastical aversion that was felt against those who were of Scottish ordination, whose forefathers were the non-jurors of the days of the Revolution, we are somewhat disposed to hesitate in accepting the judgment passed. The ten are thus described: "Peter Tustian, a stranger recently come from South Carolina, Jacob Henderson, a tory, Giles Rainsford, a stickler for the present happy establishment, John Fraser, a whig, Sam. Skippon, a whig and an excellent scholar and good man, John Colebatch, a whig and one of the best of men, James Williamson, a Scotchman, an idiot, and a tory, Daniel Maynadier, a whig and reputed a good liver, but a horrid preacher, John Donaldson, a grand tory and a rake, George Ross, a tory and belongs to the society." Nothing it will be observed is said to the disparagement of any whig except that one is said to have been a good liver, which may mean more than is expressed;

while, if it were possible to stigmatize a tory it was done. The school of Dean Swift had hardly died out yet, and it is possible that men in some degree appeared worse than they were because of the bitterness of political prejudice together with the antagonism of English and Scotch churhmen, of which latter there were always many in the colony.

The condition of things, however, was without question, bad enough. To this the testimony is very abundant. Some of the clergy also were extremely illiterate and in no way qualified for their high duties, by which also they destroyed their power for good. Marvel was even expressed how some of them could ever have obtained ordination. Maryland, by the privileges and the security it enjoyed, was made to suffer ills that other colonies escaped. The establishment was not an unmixed good.

The statement above made that the antagonism of persons had something to do in giving color to the reputation of the Maryland clergy at this time, is eminently justified in the history of the administration of the second commissary of the colony, the Rev. Jacob Henderson. The Rev. Henry Hall, the first rector of St. James' Parish, had, before Mr. Henderson, been appointed commissary of the whole colony, but had declined the honor absolutely. This was given at the time as the only reason why Gov. Hart did not suggest his name to the Bishop of London for appointment in place of Mr. Henderson. He was a man of very great force of character, and also apparently of considerable temper; as we find him, soon after coming into the parish, going to Quaker meeting, and upon being insulted, threatening to trounce the offenders. His administration of the parish was very successful, for the church eminently prospered, and there is no evidence of such wrangling and disputing as we find in subsequent periods. The congregation loved and cherished the church.

The Rev. Mr. Henderson, the new commissary, was a man not unlike Mr. Hall in temperament, but also, he was imperious and not indisposed to magnify his office; a good man, who afterwards came to be highly honored, and in the administration of his parish was highly successful; also in the use of his private fortune he was very generous. He enjoys the honor of having had erected to his memory in the church of his former cure, a commemorative window, an honor which probably Mr. Hall alone shares with him of all the clergy of that day. Though commissioned in 1715, we do not find him assuming the duties of his office till 1717. There had been no commissary since Dr. Bray's time in the colony. Mr. Henderson having convened the clergy, at the very first meeting there began a feud between these men, which continued to be a matter of disturbance for years, in the midst of which crimination and recrimination were freely indulged in. According to the record Mr. Henderson called upon the clergy present to produce their letters of ordination and license; and upon Mr. Hall's doing so the commissary put the papers in his bag, to examine them at his leisure. This Mr. Hall immediately resented, demanding the return of his property, saying, "that if the Bishop of London, or even the king himself should possess himself of his property he would resist the usurpation." The commissary refused to restore them and Mr. Hall caused a warrant to be issued for their recovery. At this, of course, Mr. Henderson was deeply offended and the whole matter was carried before the Bishop of London whom Mr. Henderson thought to be insulted in his person. The Governor of the colony and the clergy generally, took sides with Mr. Hall, the Governor particularly bearing witness to the Bishop of his great worth. The Bishop in his reply justified Mr. Hall, and promised that if Mr. Henderson should persist in being troublesome to his brethren he "would take proper means to give satisfaction, particularly to Mr. Hall, whose character I am so well pleased with."

The feud, however, reached such proportions that in 1718 when the attempt was made to strengthen the disciplinary power of the Bishop by securing the recognition of the same by the colonial legislature, it was represented to Mr. Henderson by his brethren that his cause must cease and the charges against Mr. Hall be absolutely withdrawn; probably because it was feared that if Mr. Henderson was to be the one to administer discipline for the Bishop his conduct to Mr. Hall could not commend the plan. The attempt, however, failed, and Mr. Henderson probably was largely the cause of it, for the measure had strong supporters. The commissary at this time was very unpopular with both clergy and laity, and complaints of different kinds were brought against him. His loyalty to the church was questioned, and he seems to have been generally reprehended. His difficulty with Mr. Hall for years rankled in him. Old age, however, seems at last to have mellowed his spirit and time has done much for his memory. He died in the year 1751 ; but for seventeen years he had ceased to do the duties of his office. In 1730 he had been made commissary of the whole province. He was the last one to bear the commission ; as it was found to be practically profitless for any good purpose.

It was in 1717 the commissary issued the following enquiries, prepared by the Bishop of London, which were to be answered by the church wardens under oath. They were of a nature to excite jealousy and antagonism in all quarters, and would now appear to us exceedingly unwise. Similar questions issued since our ecclesiastical independence, have excited much bitterness. These enquiries were arranged under five titles, the first of which bore upon the performance of his duties by the minister, and demanded of the church wardens whether he was of sober life and conversation, whether he was diligent in the instruction of children, whether he faithfully observed the laws and rubrics of the church, duly administered Holy Communion, gave faithful attention to the care of the parish, and read the canons, thirty nine articles, &c., as appointed. The second enquiry was about the condition and care of the church building and furniture. The third was about the morals of the people of the parish, and their attendance upon worship, and demeanor in church, and also as to persons above sixteen years old receiving the Holy Communion three times a year; for as confirmation was not administered in the colony, an age had been fixed when persons were expected to present themselves to commune. Also enquiry was made about the heads of families refusing to send their children and servants to be catechised. The fourth title covered the matter of the faithfulness of church officers, while the fifth sought into other matters, such as the faithfulness of schoolmasters where there were any, the vestry's faithfulness to their trust of tobacco on hand, and other things not included under the other heads.

Such an examination could not fail to excite much opposition, especially as it is said there was a good deal of scepticism and immorality in the colony at the time, the former particularly in high quarters; qualities that do not favor the too prying eyes of the church. Beside that, it could only excite antagonism without correcting the evil. For though the queries might be propounded they could not be made legally effective. The ordinary might through his agent learn of the trouble, of the delinquency of which the rector or the church officers might be guilty, or of the neglect of the parishioners to attend to their various duties; but there his jurisdiction ended, and as we have seen, the attempt made in the following year to secure to the Bishop power in the premises, failed. The commissary's authority therefore excited a great deal more doubt and jealousy than it did good. It was, however, in some degree a bond of union for the clergy of the colony. It brought them together from time to time. It in some measure restrained the liability of the clergy to fall into excesses.

The commissary could exhort and denounce, and so far place a delinquent rector under the ban, and in various things he could give instruction in those matters which an isolated minister, however conscientious, is apt to lose sight of. For it requires a moment's consideration to enable us to realize the condition of things at that time. The parishes were sometimes forty or fifty miles long, and in one case the report was made that the parish was forty miles square. In another instance the report states the length as sixty miles. The parishes also were sparsely settled, sometimes not averaging one family to the square mile. The clergy also were very poor as a rule, and the facilities for communication with the outside world small. In such a state of things it is readily seen that a convocation of the clergy from time to time would be a great blessing, affording intercourse with their brethern, while a commissary, who had a kind heart and good judgement, would be able to direct their attention to many things that, in the retreats of their own cures, would never occur to them. Even with our modern opportunities a convocation of the scattered ministers of a diocese, is found to be of great value in broadening the sympathies and extending the reach of thought. With no current literature, and with few standard works, (for libraries were not universal and in many cases very small), the clergy had but few of the opportunities for culture and occupation which fall to our lot. The absence of such may be one explanation of why various of them fell into unfortunate habits. Besides the standard of learning was far lower and the scrutiny into the life much less for those who would enter the ministry then than now; and many men entered holy orders who could have been kept in right courses only by the loftiest zeal or the circumstances of a high state of society. In the isolation of a Maryland parish and amidst a generally rude people it is no marvel that some fell away from rectitude. Also it will be seen that to forbid the clergy to assemble, as was afterwards done, was in every way a calamity.

CHAPTER VII.

THE PARISH.

Returning to matters more strictly parochial; from the year of the full establishment of the church we find many things that strongly attract the attention. Amongst these ranks eminently the collection of libraries which the first commissary so freely dispensed to the various parishes. These, as we have seen, varied very greatly in numbers; among the thirty given one numbering as many as a thousand and ninety-five volumes, and another only two. Others got ten, fifteen, forty, sixty, one, two or three hundred; the distribution being as far as can be perceived, without any definite rule; which was the more remarkable as the books were for the use of the minister, and therefore as much needed in one place as in another. Dr. Bray's beneficence was limited only by his ability, and he must have been controlled by circumstances of which we are now ignorant. The books were given in charge of the minister of the parish; who was to submit them from time to time to the vestry for examination. The governor also had the power to appoint a visitor to inspect; and upon the discovery of neglect or loss the rector could be sued for the damage done. Some of the books are still in existence in various places; though after having been cared for faithfully during the whole colonial period, in the days of disorder after the Revolution they became scattered and many of them have perished.

The number that came to St. James' parish in 1698 was about one hundred and fifty volumes, twenty of them being in folio, nineteen in quarto and the remainder in octavo. Most of them were in English, though a few were in Latin. Nor were they exclusively theological, but embraced also a small number of historical and scientific works. In theology, however, the collection was rich, and was as comprehensive as that number of volumes could well be made. Some of them were given by their authors, and a review of the dates of publication will surprise one at the activity of that time. What an immense convenience and comfort they were to the parochial clergy of Maryland can readily be imagined.

Previous to the reception of these books, it had been the intention of somebody to donate various books, through the governor, to the parishes, as will appear from the following section of a proclamation of January, 1697 (O. S); "I do also in his majestie's name command yt ye vestry of each respective parish return me under their hands by ye next provinciall court or sooner, a full account of what great church Bibles, common prayer bookes, and bookes of homelys they have not received from me as a gift to their parish; foure ordinary Bibles, four of ye Rev'd Doct. Williams' catechisms, sticht, as alsoe four of his Lawfullness of Common Prayer, Worship, etc., sticht, and one Whole Dutty of Man. And if they did not receive one ye Revd. Doct. Bray's Catecheticall Lectures. All persons to whom this is directed, are not to faile to comply with these my commands, as they will answer to ye contrary at theire perrill.

Signed, Ff NICHOLSON."

The vestry escaped the "perrill" by replying immediately that they had not received church Bibles or any other books from the liberality of the unknown donor.

They did, however, in 1703 receive a second invoice from the Rev. Dr. Bray, containing seventeen different lots; among which was a number of Bibles, prayer books, catechetical lectures, sermons and tracts. The tracts were for free distribution, while the Bibles, prayer books, lectures and sermons were to be put in the pews to be used by the congregation before or during service. The tracts, lectures and sermons, were of the most practical character and well adapted to the needs of the community. Nor was this the only provision made for such an object; for besides one or two smaller gifts of books we find mention made in 1709 of a legacy of twenty pounds sterling from Mr. James Rigbie, (a vestryman and otherwise a distinguished patron of the parish, as we shall see) "to be laid out in good and godly books." Whether the vestry ever recovered this amount from the executor is not so certain, for we have repeated notices of their endeavors to do so. The gift shows, however, a strong desire to counteract the existence of scepticism, and the bad influence of sceptical works ; the use of which had been fashionable in the colonies as well as in England now for many years. It shows also that the back-woods of Maryland was not a dreary waste, but that intellectually, morally and spiritually there were good men in work and prayer endeavoring to promote the cause of God and of man.

Another item of interest is the donations that were from time to time through this period made to the support and more proper ordering of the church. It would be naturally supposed that, provision being made by law, individual efforts would hardly be called out. The fact that the sheriff made his regular call upon the planter and everyone else, and demanded the tax for his family and household, would put to sleep, one would think, all more kindly consideration ; and the minister, as appointed under the law without the parishioners' consent would be left to be provided for by the law. But such was not the fact. Personal care and attention were bestowed upon the matter, so that in a report of twenty parishes, made in 1724, thirteen had glebes, others possibly might have had them had the will of the testators been in all cases carried out ; for in 1722 a bill was passed by the assembly providing that henceforth, if the purpose of the deceased could be be clearly made out from his will, any informality should not prevent the church from receiving the property devised. For glebes were almost always of private gift, though the law provided that where there was a sufficient accumulation of the clerical tax during a vacancy in the rectorship of a parish, it should be applied to the buying and stocking of glebes. Though as this was not the only use to which it could be applied, but to the building and repairing of churches as well, as was done in St. James in 1695, it is likely that but few, if any glebes were purchased. Some of these tracts of land had been given even before the act of establishment, men in the earlier desolation yearning for the preaching of the word. There are parishes in Maryland to-day that are in as full a degree or more supported by the gifts of those olden times as they are by the contributions of this present generation. In some instances indeed the present generation does nothing, the generosity of other days affording the whole support of the minister of the parish; though worse than this again, there have been generations since those times that have alienated, such church property for some passing demand rather than give of their own means for the purpose.

Among the parishes that received such substantial tokens of loving regard was St. James, and that in no scant measure. The first gift in land it received, is noticed in the year 1700, and came by will from a vestryman, James Rigbie, and his wife, the same who donated the twenty pounds sterling for books for the parish. The tract contained one hundred acres, and included what is now in the possession of the church, though forty acres have been alienated since his day. It was the loving act of husband and wife separately, each contributing one half the amount. A second donation was made of a farm of over seven hundred acres originally, known as Wrighton, lying upon the Patuxent river, the gift by will of Nicholas Turrett, also one of the first vestrymen. The will was dated 1696, though mention is first made of the land in 1719, the church having had a reversionary right according to its terms. This tract long continued in possession of the parish, though it was never apparently very profitable. It has since been sold, having dwindled away to about five hundred acres, and the proceeds invested otherwise, yielding to-day a revenue. By the terms of Mr. Turrett's will this property was left to the parish for the use of the minister, while the glebe about the church was left to the minister of the parish.

What the two legacies have been to St. James it is impossible to estimate. There have been periods in the past when the very life of the parish has been dependent upon them. Those two old men built better than they knew. The parish from the scarcity of parishioners, or from the stringency of the times, or from the lukewarmness of the people, has been occasionally almost ready to die, as some parishes in Maryland have died, or have only a name to live. The income from these sources has, however, tided it over its difficulties, and when times have brightened, has given a basis for the assurance of hope to those who loved and prized the old name and its memories, as well as the great cause of which it had always been the powerful instrument. The income has been enough to excite confidence, but never enough to cripple effort; and the result has been, that while in the rural parishes of Maryland frequent changes of ministers have taken place, St. James is marked for the comparatively long duration of the residence of many of its pastors. It is also worthy of remark that the period of such generosity was the very early one of the first decade after the passage of the first act of Establishment, and that from that day down to this, such generosity has never been emulated. The parish has had many good and excellent men, who have done their duty generously, according to the passing demand; but no one in the whole—nearly two hundred years since that time—has done anything of substantial moment for the permanent welfare of the church. Other acts of considerate affection have been done, as the gift of a bell in 1706, and various pieces of plate, as we shall hereafter see, but since the year 1700 no one has sought to associate his name with the permanent life of the parish. Why that period should have been so marked it is difficult to say. It suggests, however, that the church as established, was something very dear to the hearts of some of the people; and that there was, as all the records prove, a high degree of piety in the backwoods of Maryland, a love for the church and her ways; for worldly men do not make such contributions to the cause of religion.

We have seen how the Establishment was provided for, and the support of the clergy secured. While this in the beginning was generally acquiesced in, the Quakers and Roman Catholics alone apparently offering virulent opposition, and acquiesced in because it was recognized as being the best possible thing under the circumstances, yet as time went on and the recollection of the first benefits wore away, the system was made to encounter a good many difficulties. In the first place, trouble frequently arose between the clergy and the people, with the result of trials at law, which were made sometimes to drag on for years, or even carried by appeal to England; the result of which was, of course, an alienation between pastor and people. The members of the vestry were protected in their private estates in such suits, as was right; but the effect was, that sometimes, with unpopular men, forced upon them by the governor, they were reckless about going into such litigation, and having no personal responsibility, were a little too much disposed to hector the parsons. As it happened, they sometimes met a worthy antagonist and the result was unfortunate, as neither knew how to yield

From the very beginning such difficulties arose, though of course they frequently were easily adjusted, with good will on each side. The first rector of St. James in the commencement of his rectorship, had such a trouble. It seemed to be a feeling entertained by many of the parsons that under the law they were entitled to the whole income of the year in which they were inducted, though a portion of it had already expired when they began their ministry. The rector of St. James under this impression, claimed the whole tax for the year 1698, and the vestry, after consideration, ordered it to be paid to him, on the condition that should it be found an error of interpretation the amount would be refunded. Upon the determination of the matter the decision was in favor of the vestry, and the rector promptly complied with the agreement.

But it was not only between pastor and people that difficulties arose. It was also between the clergy and laity of the colony. For there probably never was perfect confidence on the part of either in the other, that perfect harmony that made all relations smooth. It was only the Roman Catholics who were disfranchised, and consequently there were always found in the Assembly of Maryland many non-conformists; the number in 1718 being said to be about one-third. In the beginning all such had welcomed the Establishment as the best possible thing for the colony; but now the clergy always beheld in them, and doubtless with some reason, an occasion for anxiety, believing that if in any way the friends of the Establishment became divided, this minority would be used against the Church. In the last days of the colony, when politics ran very high, such a danger became very imminent, and a great champion of the church, Mr. Boucher, had to remind certain prominent politicians that though churchmen and vestrymen, they were most inconsistently, by their influence, leagued with the force of the opposition. It was this jealousy and fear doubtless that stimulated the cry, so often raised about the time above given and afterwards, of the attempts to starve out the clergy by the division of parishes. Even the best men raised this cry. That it was without reason we may well believe, in most if not all cases; for the division of the parishes must have by this time become necessary in various portions of the colony, from the large increase of population and the demand for more places of worship, and of course more ministers. But the clergy could not always see that, and sometimes it was a great grievance, as to divide made the revenue so small that the alternative was to vacate or starve.

This minority became, also, formidable on other occasions; for unless the majority was united the balance of power was with it. But majorities are not likely to be always united. Security itself is apt to breed occasions of distraction and separation, by new issues arising. So the clergy felt and saw, and apprehended with good reason. For if it were a question of strengthening the Bishop' shands for discipline, the minority could be relied upon to prevent it. If it were a question of reducing the clergy's salary, they were trustworthy coadjutors. If it were a question of erecting a court, violating the idea of Episcopacy, for trying clergymen; the voice of the minority was ready, as they knew nothing of the idea of Episcopacy except to abominate it. And this continued through the whole period of the existence of the Establishment, so that the clergy could never enjoy perfect quietness and peace. As to the reduction of their salaries by the reduction of the tax, that was a matter never for many years truly at rest; because it was readily presented as a popular measure, the people being always desirous of a reduction in taxation. Also, it could be with great plausibility urged and defended by representing many of the salaries as excessively large, and also by seizing upon two or three unusually prosperous seasons, such as tobacco planters have from time immemorial had, when prices ranged high ; the popular mind being oblivious of the fact that such seasons are always followed by years of depression. It is true the colonial authorities attempted to prevent this variation by limiting the supply through fixing the amount, so much for each laborer, to be raised on each plantation. This probably was effective, as far as it went, for it continued to be the practice for years ; and counters were regularly appointed by the vestries, the appointing power under the law. Good care, however, was taken that the clergy should not profit by this ordinancey, for a price was fixed for commutation, so that with tobacco very high, the planters would pay over to the sheriff for the parson's use cash or grain, and with it low the tax was paid in the long leafed currency. The clergy did not, however, always have to contend alone in this matter, for the people became as much irritated against various colonial officers on account of their excessive fees, as against the clergy ; and with better reason, for charges in the various offices were generally very extravagant. A provision for commutation, then, affected them as much as it did the parsons, and without much affection, may be, for the clergy's cause, these influential men were sometimes found united with the clergy in the same battle. The difference in the value of parishes was great, some yielding from four to five times as much as others, some in 1767 paying only about one hundred pounds. while the cost of living in the matter of all things brought from abroad was very high. The clergy from time to time complained that when they were paid in tobacco it was only in the inferior grades ; for, so that it was merchantable it seems to have been receivable. We have seen how parish expenses were to be paid, by a special levy for that purpose from year to year, granted by the county court to the parish applying. The amount of this levy varied, but was never over ten pounds per poll, the amount provided for in the act of 1702. Sometimes the vestry immediately put in the application, but sometimes they acted only for parishioners who were first called upon to decide what ought to be done and what amount of tax might be necessary. The county court also had the power of granting or refusing; a liberty they sometimes exercised, in obedience possibly to some passing jealousy of the people at some supposed recklessness in the vestry. The earlier law of 1699 gave the vestry itself the power of assessing for this purpose, betraying an amount of confidence which a cooler after-judgement seems to have modified. As current expenses meant not only the keeping of the church and chapel yard in a decent and proper condition, but also renovating, restoring and rebuilding, as for instance, a vestry house when there was occasion, the amount asked for and obtained was not excessive. The whole plan of the Establishment was an economical one as compared with our later schemes ; one of its virtues being that none could shirk duty as many do now, but all had to bear a fair proportion of the burden. The only drawback was that some, though less than one-third, of the people who worshiped in other places and derived no spiritual benefit from the Establishment, had to pay a like proportion with everybody else to the

Establishment. It seemed like a hardship; though the indirect benefits in the good order and elevation of society, to which the church ministered as no other body could, doubtless compensated for any amount so levied upon nonconformists.

1698. BOOKES RECEIVED BY YE REVEREND MR.
HENRY HALL, YE――――OF MAY.

A catalogue of Bookes belonging to ye library of St. James' parish in Ann Arrundel county in Maryland, sent by ye Reverend Dr. Bray, and marked thus: belonging to ye library of Herring Creeke――――Ann Arrundel county.

BOOKES IN FOLIO—TWENTY.

PRINTED IN

1 Biblia Sacra, &c., ab imp. Tremellio
 and Fran. Juno, &c. 1603
2 Poli Synopsis Criticorum, vol. 4 in
 libr's 5 1696
3 Dr. Hammond upon ye New Testa-
 ment 1696
4 The Cambridge Concordance 1698
5 Mr. Hookers Ecclesiasticall Politie
 in 8 bookes 1682
6 Clementis Recognition: libri 10 &c.
 Opus eruditit D: Irenai: epis:
 Lugd advs, Hares: &c. lib. 5 1526
7 Dr. Jeremiah Taylor's Ductor Dubi-
 tantium 1660
8 Bishop Pearson on ye Apostles
 Creed 1683

9 Bishop Sanderson—36 Discourses,
    life and preface   1689
9 Bishop Sanderson—21 Discourses   1686
10 Philippi a Lamborch &c., Theologia
    Christiana   1695
11 A: B: Tillotson's workes   1696
12 The Jesuites Morals by Dr. Tonge   1679
13 Du Pins Ecclesiasticall History vol.
    7, books 3   1696
14 A view of Universall History from
    ye creation to ye yeare 1680 by
    Fran: Tallents
15 Thomaa Aquinatis summa totius
    Theologie in 3 P: B: 1622
16 Blomes Geography and Cosmogra-
    phy translated from Varenius and
    taken from Mons: Sanson   1693
17 Ludon: le Blane Theses Theologicæ   1683
18 Sir Richard Baker's Cronicle of ye
    Kings of England   1696
19 Q. Sept. Florentis Tertuliani opera
    qe. hactenus reperiri potuerunt
    omnia   1590
20 Dr. Bray's Catecheticall Lectures
    vol. 1st, or lectures on ye Church
    Catechism   1697

BOOKES IN QUARTO MARKED AS ABOVE.

1 Robertson: Thesaurus Grecæ linguæ   1676
2 Ejusdem Thesaurus linguæ Sanctæ   1680
3 Linguæ Romanæ luculent: novum
    Diction.   1693
4 Luijts (Johannis) Introductio ad
    Geographium   1692
5 Ejusdem Institutio Astronomica   1695

6 The Holly Bible with ye Common
   Prayer   1696
7 Francisci Turrentini Compendm.
   Theologiæ   1695
8 Vict: Bithneri Lyra Prophetica   1650
9 Dr. Parker's Demonstratio of ye law
   of nature   1681
10 Dr. Bray's Bibliotheca Parochialis   1697
11 A : B : Leighton's practicall com-
   mentary on ye first epistle generall
   of St. Peter in 2 vols. first in   1693
                         second in   1694
12 Ejusden Prælectiones Theologicæ   1693
13 Dr. Sherlock Concerning Providence   1697
14 Dr. Patrick's Parable of ye Pil-
   grime   1607
15 Lord B : p : of London-Derry Expo-
   sition on ye Ten Commandments
   with two other discourses   1692
16 A Commonplace Booke of ye Holly
   Bible   1697
17 Dr. Comber's Church History clear-
   ed from Roman forgeries   1695
18 Jonathan Stolham's Reviler rebuked   1657

BOOKES IN OCTAVO—VIZ:

1 An adridgm't of Sir Walter Ra-
   leigh's History of ye world in 5
   bookes   1698
2 The B : p : of Bath and Wells Com-
   mentary on ye 5 bookes of Moses
   in two volumes   1694
3 Dr. Sherlock on Death and Judg-
   ment   1694

4 Lovis le Comptes Memoirs and observations 1697
5 The workes of ye author of ye whole dutty of man in two volumes 1697
6 Fran: Palæopolitanus Divine Dialogues 2 volumes 1668
7 The Septuagint &c. 2 volumes 1665
8 Sanct Salvianus De Gubernatione Dei &c. 1683
9 Elis de Articulis: 39 Ecclesiæ Anglicanæ 1696
10 The plaine man's guide to Heaven 1697
11 B: p: King concerning ye invention of men in ye worship of God 169–
12 The Christian Monitor 169–
Mr. Wake's Preparation for death 168–
13 Lactantii opera omnia 168–
14 Episc: Sanderson de Obligatione Conscientiæ 169–
15 Idem de Juramento promission. 16—
16 Daniel Williams of gospell truth. 1695
17 Nath. Spinckes of Trust in God 1696
18 Reflections upon ye bookes of Holly Scripture, 2 volumes 1688
19 Mr. Dodwell's two letters of advice 1691
20 Xenophon de Institutione Cyrii Græce 1698
21 Henipin's New discovery of America 1698
22 Dr. Bates's Harmony of ye Divine attributes 1697
23 A: B: Leighton's Discourses 1692
24 Dr. Comber on ye Com'on Prayer 1609
25 An Inquirey after Happiness part ye 1st 1697
25 An Inquirey after Happiness part ye 2nd 1696

26 Part ye third by ye author of practicall Christianity   1697
27 Dr. Scott's Christian life, part ye
   first, vol 1st   1692
   and part ye second of vol. ye second   1694
28 Dr. Connant's Discourses 2 vols   1697
29 Grotius de jure Belli et Pacis   1651
30 Dr. Busbig's Græcæ Gramatices
   Rudiment.   1693
31 Dr. Jerem. Taylor of Holly Living
   and Dying   1695
32 Rays's Wisdom of God in ye
   Workes of Creation   1692
33 Dr. Pierce Pacificator: Orthodoxo
   Theolog: Corpuscul: 1685
34 B: P: Burnets Pastorall Care   1692
35 P: Lombardi Sententiarum libri:
   4: Coloniæ   1609
36 Doctor Stradlings Discourses   1692
37 Theoph: Dorington's Family De-
   votion, 4 vols.   1695
38 Amesius de Conscienta   1631
39 Dr. Bray of ye Baptismal Covenant   1697
40 Dr. Falkner's Vindication of Litur-
   gies   1681
41 His Libertas Ecclesiastica   1683
42 Ye B: P: of Bath & Wells on ye
   Church Catechism   1686
43 Clerici Ars Critica   1698
44 Doct Barron on ye Apostles Creed   1697
45 The Snake in ye Grass   1698
46 B: p: Stillingfleet Concerning
   Christ's Satisfaction   1697
47 His Vindication of ye Doctrine of
   ye Trinity   1697

48	His Discourses, 2 volumes	1697
49	A Discourse Concerning Lent in 2 parts	1696
50	William Wilson of Religion and ye Resurrection	1694
51	Dr. Ashton Concerning Deathbed-Repentance	1696
52	H. Stephani Catechismus Græco-Latinus	1604
53	Biblia Vulgata p. Robertum Stephanum	1555
54	The Life and Meditations of M: A: Antoninus R; Emp.	1692
55	Abbadies Vindication of ye Trueth of Xtian Religion part 1st	1694
—	Abbadies Vindication of ye Trueth part 2d.	
56	The Practicall believer, in two parts	1688
57	Wingates Arithmetic	1694
58	Sr. Math. Hales Contemplations Morall and Divine in 2 parts	1695
59	Fran: Buggs Picture of Quakerism in 2 parts	1697
60	W. A. of Divine Assistance	1698
	His Christian Justification stated	1670
	His Animadversions on yt p.t of Robt. Ferguson's book, entitled ye Interest of Reason in Religion which treats of Justification	1676
61	His Serious and Friendly Address to ye Non-conformists	1693
—	His State of ye Church in Future Ages	1684
—	The Mystery of iniquity Unfolded	1675
62	W: A: Catholicisme	1683

— The Danger of Enthusiasm Discovered 1674

63 { W. A. of Humility 1681
Of ye nature, series and order of Occurences 1689
His pursuasion to Peace and Unity among Xtians 1680

64 The First. ⎫
65 The Second. ⎬ volumes of A: B: p: Tillotson's Discourses pub. by Dr. Baker
66 The Third. ⎬
67 The Fourth. ⎭
                  1698
                  1696
                  1696
                  1697

— Dr. Tillotson's Rule of Faith 1670
68 Dr Stillingfleet's Reply to J. S. 3rd Appendix &c 1675
69 The Unreasonable: of Atheisme made Manifest 1669
70 Dr. Hammond de Confirmatione 1665
71 Dr. Wake, Concerning Swearing, Duplicate 1696
72 His Discourses on Severall Occasions 1697
73 Dr. Cockburn's Fifteen Discourses 169–
73 Ascetecks or ye Heroick vertue of ye Ancient Christian Anchorites and Cænobites 1691
74 Theologica Mistica: 2 Discourses Concerning Devine Communication to Souls Duly Disposed 1697
75 Dr, Goodman's Seven Discourses 1697
76 Dr. Horneck's Severall Discourses upon ye fifth chapter of Matthew, vol. ye 1st. 1698
77 Dr. Pelling's Discourse upon Humility 1694
78 Concerning Holliness 1695
79 Concerning ye Existence of God 1696

80	Jno. Ketlewells Help and Exhortation to Worthy Communicating	1696
81	His Five Discourses on Practicall Religion	1696
82	His Measures of Christian Obedience	1696
83	Dr. Hody of ye Resurrection of ye Same Body	1694
84	Grotins de Veritate Religionis Christiana	1675
85	Mr. John Edwards' Thoughts Concerning ye Severall Causes and Occasions of Atheism	
86	His Socinianism Unmasked	1696
—	His Discourse Concerning ye Authority, Stile, and perfection of ye	
87	Old & New Testament, in three vol:	1696

(Spelling and Style as in the Original.)

CHAPTER VIII.

OTHER ITEMS.

There are various items that suggest themselves at this period of the history which can hardly be brought forward as well at any later time, some of them of moment as parochial matters, and some having a broader interest. Amongst them is the care that was bestowed by the colonial legislature, through almost the whole period of its continuance, to provide for the morals of the people and for their right religious views. We have noticed the Act of 1649; and though all honor is to be done to Maryland for the lead it assumed thereby in the great cause of toleration, yet privilege was only extended by it under the then generally recognized standard of orthodoxy, and all those who came short of that, those, for instance, that denied the Divinity of Our Lord, or the doctrine of the Trinity, were denied its benefit. Such views now do not debar a man from claims to be a religious man or even to be a christian, and they who hold such views set themselves up to be the liberal men of the day. But in 1649, by the instrument then passed, such persons were regarded as blasphemers, and were amenable to all the penalties for that crime. They were disloyal to the Almighty and traducers of their Lord, and their punishment was greater than if they had used the foulest language or done the most immoral deed. And so also at the period to which we have now come. By a law of 1723 blasphemy is defined, to maliciously and wilfully curse God, "to deny the Saviour to be the Son of God, to deny the Holy Trinity, or the Divinity of the several persons of the Trinity;" and for this the punishment was, for the first offence boring through the tongue, the guilty member, and a fine of twenty pounds sterling, or imprisonment for six months; for the second offence branding in the forehead with the letter B and a fine of forty pounds sterling, or imprisonment for twelve months; and for the third offence the punishment was death. The thunders of the secular power were heavy enough, though it is doubtful whether the bolt did any very serious execution; rather a *brutum fulmen*, so that men might make it as loud as they pleased. For profane swearing, also, the fine was heavy, being for the first offence two shillings and sixpence, and for the second, five shillings. Drunkards also were fined. By the law of 1692, Sabbath breaking was punished by a fine of one hundred pounds of tobacco, to go to the poor; and ordinary keepers who on that day might sell liquor, except in case of necessity, or who might permit tippling on their premises, were liable to pay two hundred pounds. By the law of 1723 the guilt of profane swearing was especially deep if it were done in the presence of a vestryman, church warden, or other parties named; and also the guilt of drunkenness, the punishment being not only a fine, but also, if the party were not a "freeholder or other reputable person," whipping or the discomfort of the stocks. The observance of Sunday also was strictly required by this law, and work, gaming, fishing, fowling, hunting and other forms of diversion, were strictly forbidden; also the sale of "strong liquors;" so early have we provision for that respect for the Lord's day which has always honored Maryland. Ministers were commanded to read this law publicly four times a year; and they, or the magistrates refusing to carry out its provisions, were themselves fined. By this law, which was indeed excessively severe in some of its clauses, is shown the resolution of Maryland to promote the elevation of her people; and it shows also that there was among the people a great commanding sentiment in behalf of the ordinances and proprieties of the christian life. The law was passed about twenty-eight years after the church as an Establishment had been at work; and witnesses to the high standard which by its influence had been created among the population. It will be remembered also that this was in a time when the church had had to endure very much opposition. Her influence in spite of the antagonism had evidently been great and blessed.

A less satisfactory subject of observation is the treatment which they received who were thought to believe too much, Roman Catholics, whose affiliations over and beyond the gospel, were supposed to be equally dangerous with blasphemy and to imperil the state. We have seen how they were brought under the ban when the

Protestant Revolution overthrew the old order of things. Every other form of positive belief could be tolerated except theirs; though for them evidently the law of 1649 had been passed. William III. made the existence of the law of 1702 to be contingent upon the avowal of the principle of toleration; and in 1706, by the colonial action, the principle was enlarged in its expression. For the Roman Catholics, however no abundant grace was found, and that for every reason; because they were dreaded politically, and abominated for their false theological views. Their theological views also were feared because they were supposed to be their political guide, and that they could not with them be loyal to the state; doubtless a great misconception, but unfortunately very widely prevalent. For in periods of great agitation in secular affairs in England the Roman Catholics have always been found loyal. Patriotism has proven stronger than doctrinal views.

After the Protestant Revolution, a severe law was passed in 1704, entitled an act to prevent the growth of popery within the province. Under this act all Bishops or priests of the Roman Catholic Church were inhibited, by severe penalties, from saying mass or exercising the spiritual functions of their office, or endeavoring in any manner to persuade the inhabitants to become reconciled to the Church of Rome. Also members of that church were prohibited from engaging in the instruction of youths. Relief, however, in some measure followed immediately from the stringency of these provisions; for at the same session of the Assembly liberty was granted the priests of exercising spiritual functions in private families of the Roman Church; a relief that was continued from that time onward. A severe enactment also was passed in 1715, by which if a protestant father should die, leaving children, and his widow should be a Roman Catholic, or marry a Roman Catholic, it was possible for the Governor and council, upon application, to remove such children from the custody of their mother "to save them from popery." They were also to be educated out of their father's estate. In 1729 the county court had this jurisdiction. Evidently the thought was that the mother had no inherent rights in her children; and also that after the father the children pre-eminently belonged to the state, and that the state was the guardian of the children for their highest welfare after the father. The dread and hatred of popery as pestilential to the commonwealth and deadly to the soul, could hardly be more strongly expressed. The spirit of persecution had certainly then not died out. There are various social propositions which we regard as obsolete, contained in that act, which after a hundred and fifty years, fill us with amazement. It was passed, however, at a time when the name of Roman Catholic was, however unworthily, associated with the thought of rebellion.

Later on, in 1716, after the attempt of the Pretender upon the throne of England, test oaths that had been required of all persons holding office in the colony, were re-enacted, and amongst them the declaration in respect of transubstantiation. This of course prevented the Roman Catholic from holding office, and the exclusion from public life was rendered the more complete by a law of 1718 by which such test oaths and declaration could, upon a person being suspected of being a Roman Catholic, be administered as a qualification for voting. This finished their disfranchisement, a burden under which they rested down to the close of the colonial period. Dread and jealousy were always felt towards them, which in many ways made their position painful. Yet it did not apparently affect their numbers, the ratio of which to the whole population, remaining about the same. Nor did their priests cease to be active or to make converts, one of the charges, repeatedly made, being that irregularity of life in the parsons favored priests, proselyting zeal. Also the clergy, in addressing Gov. Hart in 1714, desired the repression of the Papists and other dissenters, who were accused of abusing their liberty under the law; an appeal that doubtless found willing ears. For in addition to the other means used for this purpose which we have seen, as early as 1708 there was a tax imposed of twenty shillings per poll upon all Irish servants of that faith brought in, "to prevent the growth of Papacy;" a law that was subsequently re-enacted several times. Other articles taxed in the same ordinance were negro slaves and rum.

Another act of discrimination and equally reprehensible according to our notions, was the attempt, though it failed, to lay a double burden on Roman Catholics to meet the expenses of the French war, a measure that, though it had a general bearing, was thought rather to be aimed at certain particular individuals. Nor did it fail because there was seen to be any special injustice in it, but because the whole project, of which it was a part, failed ; the occasion being one of the earlier and more vigorous struggles of the people against prerogative.

There was indeed a consistent plan pursued of expressing abhorrence of the Roman Catholic Church through the colonial period from the days when the Roman Catholic Lord Baltimore, was deprived, a plan that had its origin and expression in the abhorrence that was conscientiously felt. And unfortunately for the members of that church, both in England and in the colonies the fires of religious antagonism were kept burning by almost every leading consideration of the time. The reigning family of England was of the Protestant Succession, while the Pretender was of the Roman church. England was strongly protestant, while France, of which there was continual jealousy and which was supporting the Pretender, was Roman Catholic. Besides, though the Roman pontiff is now, and has for many years been recognized as having but small political influence, particularly in those states with which England is brought into close contact, in the last century his power was supposed to be great, and doubtless was so. England, though she felt her way carefully towards Roman Catholic emancipation for many years, was not able to pass the Relief Bill till 1829, when disabilities, in the presence of which all those in the colony were almost as nothing, were finally in great part removed. Intolerance born of fear, died very hard. While the Pope of Rome along with his inordinate claims to depose princes, and condemn them to death, to exercise temporal jurisdiction in the various states and kingdoms, to appoint heretics to death, and to bind the consciences of his followers to carry out his decrees, was supposed to have power to make these claims effective, there is no wonder that his name was dreaded, and that all that could become his instruments, were looked upon with suspicion. Self preservation itself demanded restrictive measures. It was the misfortune of the times; and while individuals were to be pitied, the church itself was the chief cause of their annoyances and discomforts. It ill becomes us now to avow a mock sentiment in regard to the matter, as even some Protestant writers are disposed to do, clerical as well as lay; thinking that it belongs to their modern liberality. Judge men of the olden times by the force of the circumstances of those olden times. The lawyers, merchants, and planters of a hundred and fifty years ago, had been moulded by a great combination of facts; and their jealousies and anxieties, which we are glad to have outgrown, were then but natural.

If our Maryland ancestors had a good deal of puritanical zeal, as exibited in their care for the Lord's day and their antagonism against unbelief or misbelief, as well as their regard for the proprieties of life in the matter of drinking, swearing and licentiousness, for all which they attempted to provide by their laws; they exhibited a good deal of fortitude also, and braved circumstances in coming to the house of God that would appal their successors of this day. A celebrated author has recently said that the art of keeping warm is of modern invention, a fact which will require no argument to demonstrate. And eminently was the absence of this art seen in the house of God. For down till about two generations ago the churches of Maryland had no fires in them, nor any means provided for making a fire. So that the worshipers of that day had to sit through the long service and sermon, (and without the responses by the people and the singing of the anthems, it must have seemed very long), and shiver. Their rides were often many weary miles, and the roads unspeakably bad, but yet they were found at their place. There was fire in the vestry house, which was a detached building, and doubtless there was in the capacious fireplace there a roaring flame from the logs of the abundant forrest. But at church time they rigidly withdrew to the sanctuary, turning the key in the door to prevent all access to the cheerful blaze, and ordering the sexton to permit no one to enter. There is only one explanation to give of their ability and willingness to endure this, that they were not much accustomed to warmth at home ; for with their small houses, such as were almost universal in the earlier days, the door was almost always open in the sitting room, and heat was secured not by shutting out the blast but by piling on more fuel. They roughed it, as the saying is, and those that were strong enough to stand the roughing, were able to sit in church or anywhere else and not perish. Our standard of comfort is of very modern creation, and even we look back with some wonder how our fathers of a generation ago were able to endure their discomforts patiently. For Maryland habits have been very odd, as witness the experience of the owner of a large plantation whose kitchen was on the opposite side of the public road from the house. One afternoon in summer, we are told, her friends gathered together to partake of her hospitality, but as evening drew near a most violent thunder storm came on, with a drenching rain; and as the tinder box, and fire, and supper were all across the way hostess and guests had to sit in quietness and hunger and darkness far into the night, till the storm had passed away. They were a sturdy set though, nevertheless, and their comforts, such as they were, were like their principles, more liberal than those they left behind them in the mother country.

The item of stocks is frequently mentioned in the vestry records of those times, not bank or railroad, though the vestry often had funds to invest, but that peculiar institution contrived to make poor delinquents very uncomfortable. Once also the whipping post is mentioned, an order being passed that one should be set up. This was in 1747. But from the beginning the stocks are frequently mentioned. The vestry also paid for the same out of the parish funds, an account being rendered the vestry in the year 1708. They were probably erected as a neighborhood convenience for miscreants in general; they were also, however, regarded as valuable for church discipline: for in 1765 the rule was made by the vestry that persons intruding into pews belonging to others and refusing to withdraw, should be put in the stocks, and a pair was ordered to be set up near the church. It would appear from this that the vestries had more than the power of preserving order about the church; for to do that an offender need only be held for trial. They did execute the decrees of the county court in cases of immorality, and also they had the power of action in other cases, as admonishing those living in guilt, which implied that they had the power of summoning witnesses and requiring the presence of the accused. This case would seem to indicate that they exercised some of the old manorial right of holding a petty court. The parish was for certain purposes to them as a manor, and in offences against good morals and the violation of peace during the time of worship and the infringement of private rights within the precincts of the house of God, they had power. The ducking stool, the pillory and branding irons were also institutions of Maryland, but not in the hands of the vestry.

Why a halo should be supposed to surround a church because it was built of English brick, it would be difficult to say. Such, however, is the fact; for there is hardly an old church in Maryland built during the colonial period that is not said to have been so erected. Yet the assertion is true of very few. Most of the brick churches in Maryland were built just before the revolution when there was an abundance of skill in Maryland; while the clay in very many parts of the state is of excellent quality. Also, though English goods were high, yet labor in Maryland was low. Why, therefore, people should have gone to England to buy what they could get as good and cheaper at home, is a difficult question.

Nor does the size of the bricks indicate anything, for the mechanic, having learned his trade in England, would of necessity almost, use the same mould he had been accustomed to, and also the same process of manufacture. Also, even though granting the charges of freight were nothing, which is doubtful, yet the cost of handling and carrying, perhaps for miles, would be excessive over and above that of bricks made where they were needed. The tradition, therefore, is probably hardly ever reliable. As early as 1717 we find the vestry of St. James' parish ordering, and in 1718 paying for twenty thousand bricks made upon the glebe; and the high probability is that as this church stood as near to a port as most of the parish churches, when the time came to erect its substantial walls, the contractor went to the same pit for his clay and from that built this memorial of the Maryland churchman's confidence.

Our forefathers in the church did not hold the use of liquor in abomination as some of their descendants of this time are disposed to do. It is true that St. James' parish was the field on which the first local option law operated, but it was not for Maryland churchmen. The Quakers who abounded among them, were grievously afflicted at their meetings by the resort of "evil and wicked" persons thither to sell strong drink; and as early as 1702 they appointed a committee to wait on the Governor and Council to seek an abatement of the nuisance. This was promised them, but again in 1711 they made the same complaint, and in 1725 an act was passed by the Assembly to prevent the sale of liquor within two miles of the meeting house at West River. It is not on record how far the Friends were total abstainers themselves, and so differed from their fellow citizens. The churchmen, however, of that day have left no record of their abomination, in any way, of ardent spirits, but rather we find under the date of 1703 an order passed by the vestry for two gallons of rum for the use of the men engaged in underpinning the church, a large amount of rum certainly for a small amount of work. The raising and underpinning implied a large gathering, and the rum was to promote jollity as well as activity; and, of course, on such an occasion all the vestry were present. This explains the generous supply. It is not on record, however, that the vestry of St. James' had a standing order for the sexton to provide "a quart of rum and sugar equivalent, and as much diet as would give the vestry a dinner," though such was the rule of a parish in Baltimore county until a loud protest was made. Then their rum and diet had to be provided at their private charges. We are not informed whether their zeal flagged on that account; though it is likely that previously their meetings had been exceedingly well attended, and that without fear of the impending fine, which in other places was thought to be sufficient but necessary.

A review of the parish from this point suggests satisfactory consideration. The church was well filled with a constantly increasing congregation, occasioned partly by an increasing population, though also by an increasing interest in holy things in the people. The population did increase very much, as in 1696 the number of taxables was five hundred and seven, and in 1725 eight hundred and seven, three hundred in about thirty years. This of course includes the servants who were taxables, and probably only a small ratio was of new families come in. There was probably not a great increase from that source, as it was a new country but recently taken up, and the planters would hardly be disposed to divide or part with their land; while also new settlers had plenty of new country to go out to, where the cost would be much less. Increase in population, therefore, meant rather increase in prosperity among the planters, that is, the increase of servants. The parish also was at peace, and the rector and people harmonious. There is no evidence that the then rector's difficulties with the commissary were even known to the people. The income of the rector also was ample; for beside the proceeds of the tax which came almost entirely to him, and which would have yielded at least six hundred dollars of our money, on an average of seven hundred polls, he had the income from the two glebes. Other perquisites also fell to his portion, among them, it would seem, the mulatto children that were born of free women. For these were claimed by the clergy, and in one instance seemingly the claim was allowed in Mr. Hall's favor. He was apparently also a gentleman of considerable private means, from the lands that belonged to him; for it was not only the disappointed or the penniless that came to Maryland; but while the love of adventure brought some, others doubtless were swayed by the highest Christian motives.

All the officers of the parish, too, took an interest in their duties, and apparently attended to them faithfully. About 1720 a pressure was put upon them and delinquents were fined for absence, as much as one hundeed pounds of tobacco, worth from two to three dollars. In one instance the rector himself was fined, for there was no respect of persons, and he was "principal vestryman." The churches generally would present rather an odd appearance to our eyes, with the various distinctions that were made in their sittings. For beside the rector's pew there were the warden's and the vestrymen's pews, to which only they, or strangers by invitation, could go, and there was the private gallery erected by private families at their own expense. There were also the men's pews and the women's pews, evidently the free seats, and beside this, in some churches there were appointed places for slaves. Some of the churches had bells which continued to be used down to the Revolution, when some of them disappeared; tradition says, broken up to be moulded into cannon to utter the voice of destruction, in place of their former invitation to praise and prayer. The surplice with the stole is the only vestment mentioned throughout the colonial period.

How far the church had wrought a good influence in the community, it is diffiuclt to say. It is observable that certain crimes indicating a low degree of moralty, or rather a very degraded class in the parish, had in a large measure apparently ceased. Possibly, of course, the vestry had become lax in the execution of the law, though this is hardly possible. A high state of morality had probably grown up, and the degraded classes had in a measure become reformed. In 1733, however, we find the reappearance of the same enormities. A law passed in 1715 and re-enacted in 1717 and 1728 would show that in various parts of the colony there was a very abandoned set, the creation and result doubtless in a large measure of that body of convicts that were emptied out upon these shores year by year by the "mother" country.

The church, however, was not the only good influence at work. The Quakers, we have seen, were very strong in this part of Maryland, and especially in St. James' parish, and their first yearly meeting in America was here. Also their greatest strength lay at points remote from the parish church where the influence of the rector and the church administration would, from their central location be less felt, that is, along the shore of the bay from North to South. The Friends had a meeting house in each direction, and doubtless did much to improve the morals and elevate the religious tone of the community. For the Quaker of that day, with his decided and clear doctrines, was a much more influential factor than his brother of to-day, who, as a follower of Elias Hicks, has so little that is positive to guide him. There were also some Roman Catholic priests, who were allowed full influence upon the plantations of those of their own name, and doubtless they helped to ameliorate the condition of the community. They had sufficient liberty to excite the anxiety of the rectors of parishes, and if the later fathers were as devoted as the ealier missionaries they were in many ways a blessing. Of other forms of church ministration apparently there was none.

How far St. James' parish was a fair index to the general condition of the colony it is difficult to say. There appears scarcely any general reason why it should not be so accepted; and if it was, notwithstanding all that has been said to the contrary, Maryland can only be regarded as having been particularly fortunate. Church ministration was secured to her; and all other Christian bodies, though the Roman Catholic only in a limited degree, were allowed liberty. By the first a great and immovable barrier was fixed to the flood of grossness and licentiousness that had before flooded the colony, and by it, assisted by the other christian bodies, that flood was forced ever within narrower limits, and society delivered from its desolation. Of that other and far higher benefit, wrought in the heavenly ministration, by which individual souls were fed with the Bread of Life, it is impossible to speak. The Establishment secured for the colony what it never had before, and what otherwise it would not have had, the regular, faithful and consistent service of God's ordained ministry; and thus only was it or could it have been delivered from spiritual ruin.

CHAPTER IX.

THE SECOND RECTORSHIP.

THE CHURCH IN ENGLAND.

With the period commencing with the year 1722 to which we have now come, there are associated many particulars interesting, not because they are pleasing to contemplate, but because they present certain aspects of church life greatly in contrast with our own. The church in England was at this time passing through great trials; for after the death of Queen Anne in 1714, who was devoted to the church, and under whom churchmen were favored, whose reputation also in America was fostered by various gifts to the parishes, there arose by patronage of the first of the Georges, an entirely new class of men, professing latitudinarian views of an extreme type, and as much as possible depreciating church authority. How far this was the outgrowth or reaction from the Jacobite tendencies of the High Church party, cannot be said; but certain it is, the state favored the new school, recognizing its members as safer instruments for its purposes; and they obtained a large part of its patronage, being given the most eminent positions in the gift of the government.

In harmony with this was the principle on which the government was administered by Sir Robert Walpole. His determination was to preserve everything in quietness, regarding the internal prosperity of the state as being the highest consideration for an officer of the government. Acting on this principle he refined down differences, he avoided in legislation every thing that might irritate one or the other of the great classes into which society was divided, the church and non-conformists. Where he could not directly do away with the obstacles to peace, he temporized, as in some of the older repressive laws enacted after the Restoration; and either violations of the laws were overlooked, or else their operation was suspended for a season. This policy had begun before Walpole became Prime Minister, but after he had become influential in the government on the accession of George I.; and it continued to be the policy throughout his long administration, and afterwards.

Among other things done during this time was the suspension of convocation in 1717, chiefly because it had dared to raise its voice against the growth of extreme latitudinarian views as set forth by the Bishop Hoadly of Bangor. Convocation had been the church's appointed and legal means of expressing its views and desires upon matters of its own concern, and was the great preservative agent of the church against laxity of views and practice. The Bishop of Bangor's views were offensive in the extreme, contending as he did, "against the notion of the existence of any visible church, and scoffing at the maintenance of tests of orthodoxy and the claims of ecclesiastical government." Convocation protested against such views, with the result that it was prorogued, either because the government did not want agitation in the kingdom, or because the whole school to which Bishop Hoadly belonged, were regarded as being more favorable to whig principles.

This policy had a very pernicious influence upon the condition of the church. Discipline ceased, and laxity both in doctrine and practice became common. We have often heard of the fox hunting parsons of the eighteenth century, but fox hunting was not the only thing in which remissness was shown. The whole tone of the clergy sank. There was nothing to regulate or define doctrine or practice. Men were exalted to station, not because they were fitted for it either by learning or devotion, but because they were in harmony with the prevailing principles of the government, and might be useful to the party in power. One result of this condition of things, was the great agitation upon the doctrine of the Trinity, in which Dr. Waterland bore such a leading part, and at this time an attempt was made even so to alter the Prayer Book as to make it harmonize with Arian tenets. Deism also had its strong advocates, and the religion of nature was set up as the antagonist sufficient to displace christianity. It was this controversy that called out in defence of the truth Bishop Warburton in his Divine Legation of Moses, and Bishop Butler in his Analogy. It was a time of extreme agitation, everything Christian being impugned, frequently by those who held the honors and emoluments of the church.

And practice tallied with laxity in principle. Residence by the Bishops in their dioceses, in some instances when we would least expect it, was felt to be a burden, and was avoided as much as possible. The church was not felt to be a living body. Truth was more a matter of philosophy than a guide of life; while practical precepts were rather moral apothegms than the voice of the Master and Savior calling, This is the way, walk ye in it. So far had the church lost her vitality that when Secker, who became Archbishop in 1758, attempted to send over bishops to the American colonies, he found himself antagonized by the church to that degree that he had to abandon his intention. The church had become only the creature of the state for certain functions, the contests of her members were often only the battles of philosophers for certain ideas; spiritually she was cold.

One result of this was inevitable. The tone of the clergy and people fell. We hear a good deal about the condition of the clergy in the colonies, and many were painfully derelict, though there has been a very great deal of exaggeration. It was not America, however, that was alone so afflicted. For we find in a description of the clergy of England at this time, that they figured as "courtiers, politicians, lawyers, merchants, usurers, civil magistrates, sportsmen, musicians, stewards of county squires and tools of men in power." They were completely secularized, lived as men of the world, with all the deadening influence of such connection. Their separation was a lost fact; and with the loss there was the depreciation of character. The social position of the clergy was then very different from what it is now, and with the difference there was less to restrain them. A clergyman now has many more safeguards thrown around him; for as a class, from the highest to the lowest, his calling makes him the equal of any other class, and gives him a defined position, which it is easy for him to keep if he will, and which he sacrifices at his peril. All men honor his calling, all men take it for granted that he honors it, as the vast majority of his brethren do, and so none look down upon him or despise him. And all this is a great moral influence about him, irrespective of other considerations, to support him in his position.

Just the opposite was the case in that day and before. For according to a picture drawn by Dean Swift, in the days of Queen Anne, "the recognized social position of a clergyman and his family was about that of a tradesman. He made no attempt to keep up the status of a gentleman. 'The vicar' says he, 'will probably receive presents now and then from his parishioners, and perhaps from his squire, who although he may be apt sometimes to treat his parson a little superciliously, may probably be softened by a little humble demeanor. The vicar is likewise generally sure to find, on his admittance to the living, a convenient house and barn in repair, with a garden and a field or two to graze a few cows and one horse for himself and his wife. He has a market probably very near him, perhaps in his own village. No entertainment is expected by his visitor beyond a pot of ale and a piece of cheese. His wife is little better than goody in her birth, education or dress, and as to himself, he must let his parentage alone. If he be the son of a farmer it is very sufficient, and his sister may decently be chambermaid to the squire's wife. He goes about on working days in a grazier's coat and will not scruple to assist his workmen in harvest times. His daughters shall go to service, or be sent apprentice to the sempstress in the next town, and his sons are put to honest trades."

Nor is this picture of clerical life isolated, the representation of one sour-tempered man. There is abundance of proof that the better social standing of the parochial clergy is of later times. One of the laws of Queen Elizabeth's time prescribes rules for the clergy in marrying, one of which was "that no priest or deacon should marry without the approbation first obtained of the Bishop and two justices of the peace for the county, nor without the consent of the parents or relatives of the woman, or of the master or mistress with whom she was at service, in case she had no relatives." Also, we have some pictures of clerical life in the last century subsequent to this date, one of which, recently published and exceedingly beautiful, is supposed to have suggested to Goldsmith, in some of its features, the Vicar of Wakefield. At that time the condition of the parochial clergy in England, whatever it may be now, was humble. By his office the curate could claim nothing, though a godly life has always been a power.

In America, doubtless, the relative position of the clergy in society was higher. This would necessarily result from the much simpler ways of living in the colonies, and from the fact that the population was composed in such large proportion of those who came to this country with but little, and whose fortunes were made by themselves; though it is true that many of the higher orders of society did emigrate from England, and make their homes here. Still, there was always a far nearer approach to equality. In the northern colonies, where there was an ambition for as near an approach to a theocracy as possible, of course the ministers were awarded all honor and esteem; but in the southern colonies there may have been present some of that English feeling to account for the harsh language and the want of consideration that at times manifested themselves and strongly in the period to which we have now come. Individual men may have been highly respected, as certainly they were; but when from any cause they combined and stood forth as a body, to proclaim any principle or to maintain any right, there was nothing in the general esteem for their office or position to compel men to treat them with consideration; and further, the faults and shortcomings of a few would, in the popular imagination and language, be charged against the whole body as a class.

All these causes, however, united, the low esteem, socially, in which the clergy were held, their being mixed up in the political agitations of the day, when every man was distinguished as a Tory and Jacobite, or a Whig and friend of the Hanoverian succession, the taking away from the church the power of regulating her own internal affairs when the mouth of Convocation was closed and all power of discipline suspended; fearfully depressed the Church both at home and in the colonies, paralyzed her efforts, depreciated her standard, lowered her in the regard of the world, caused the truth, which she held in trust, to be questioned and rejected, and made iniquity to abound. And in proportion as these causes operated in England they affected America.

But while the Church in the Mother Country could not at this time raise her head proudly before the world by reason of the lethargy of her children, and because of the want of harmony in regard even to the most important matters of the faith, her condition was not without its hopeful and its redeeming features. For if some of her children questioned the living truths and denied the great Christian principles, there were many through this century whose writings and whose lives presented in the strongest light the natural hold the Church has upon all the living principles of truth and godliness. Some of these great men have been mentioned, as Waterland, Butler, and Warburton, men of commanding force and discrimination; while there also flourished Jones of Nayland, Samuel Wesley, the father of John and Charles, William Law, and Bishop Wilson, men who combined with learning a piety and devotion that have given them an undying name. At this time also there were various religious societies connected with the church in different parts of England, which by their association kept alive a religious spirit and proved instruments for kindling the piety of such men as the Wesleys and Whitfield. Also in 1729 the Society of Methodists was first formed at Oxford, composed of members of the Church of England. Among the original members were other men as prominent as the Wesleys; for the society had as its original intention to promote the piety of the members themselves. For this purpose they assembled every night to review their individual lives of the past, day and to build themselves and each other up in truth and godliness, by the study of the scriptures and prayer. Further than this, their work was to instruct, as they had opportunity, their associates in the University, and to teach in the schools, work houses, and prisons, wherever indeed they might find an opening.

Thus began the movement that has accomplished such vast results, not only in England but throughout the world, the work of men who were rigid in the observance of all rules and ordinances of the Church of England, and whose piety not only burned, but was kindled at her altars. So that though the condition of the Church in England was bad at the time we are in, yet her future and glorious resuscitation was already preparing, the ashes of the phenix were already stiring with life. For it was out of this Methodist movement, though in its later stages, but before separation took place from the English Church, that the evangelical school sprang, with the great names of Cecil, Conyers, Venn, Milner, and Simeon at its head; which did more than any other body of men or any other school of teaching, to work the great revival, in the calm steady heat of which the whole Anglican communion flourishes to-day. Other influences have since manifested themselves, but that both anticipated their day, had its own peculiar work for the promotion of piety and good works, and prepared the way for the entrance of these other agencies.

CHAPTER X.

THE CHURCH IN AMERICA.

A general review of ecclesiastical affairs in America would reveal, that with the growth of years there had been a general enlarging of the spirit of liberty. The question, What had brought it about? might be answered differently according as men looked with the spirit of calm investigation upon the matter, seeking only the truth, or as they were filled with admiration for the people of any given section of the country. The readiest reason, however, reached for the great change in public sentiment would probably be, that religion had not so strong a hold on men's minds and hearts, that in the one hundred years that had elapsed since the establishment of the earlier colonies, when men sought a refuge from religious intolerance, where they might themselves show equal if not greater intolerance, the ardor of their own minds had sensibly cooled down, the distinct lines of an ecclesiastical republic had been made less distinct by a freer spirit of civilization, by the influence of trade, education, and the apprehension of civil rights. New England outgrew a commonwealth founded on Mosaic law, as Israel had done so long before. This larger spirit of administration, was strikingly exemplified in the treatment of the Quakers. For during the rule of Governor Belcher, which began in 1729, Massachusetts passed a law "making satisfaction to the posterity of those who endured capital punishment in the years 1658 and 1659; and the same Assembly decreed a compensation to the decendants of the unfortunate victims of the prosecutions for witchcraft in 1693." Also, "the Legislature of Connecticut in 1729 passed an act for exempting Quakers and Baptists from ecclesiastical taxes, and in 1731 a similar law was enacted by the Assembly of Massachusetts," in which they were eminently ahead of Maryland and Virginia.

What had helped, however, to bring about this change was the difference in the spirit of the home government towards the colonies, and particularly towards those of New England. For while in their earlier days the troubles in England secured to them very great licence, and they were able to conduct their affairs after their own wills; and then had every encouragement to do so by the success which attended their friends in the Rebellion, being fortified in every claim and pretension by the supremacy to which Independency had attained; after the Restoration, and the complete overthrow of the ecclesiastical system of the commonwealth, royal injunctions and commands were heard which had to be obeyed, and toleration of almost all classes came to be the rule. The hated prelacy, against which New England puritanism had protested as against sin, raised its temples in the strongholds of the faith; and the Prayer Book, with all its papistical ceremonies, guided and directed the worship of many of the most esteemed citizens. The dawn of the eighteenth century was the breaking forth of the brightest spirit of civil and religious liberty that ever glorified the world, though that spirit shone in its brightness over a territory that extended but little beyond the realms of the happier empire of Protestant England.

It was before our present date that the examination began at Yale College into the grounds and claims of Episcopacy, that resulted in the conviction in the minds of its rector and one of its tutors, and also of Dr. Sam. Johnson, a congregational minister and friend of the rector, that Episcopacy was the true scriptural form of church government, and that no orders were valid that were not episcopally conferred. The result of this conviction was, that they all resigned their positions, and going to England were received into the ministry of the church. Two of them afterward returned to America, death intervening to prevent the third, and they ministered as missionaries of the Society for Propagating the Gospel, occupying for many years positions of commanding influence, and compelling the hearing of the church's claims.

This society was at that time the chief hope of the church in all parts of America, Maryland and Virginia excepted. It was the missionary organization of that day, as it still is in very large measure in the Church of England, though its labors are now supplemented by the Church Missionary Society, the child of the Evangelical movement at the close of the eighteenth century. Its revenue was the free will offerings of the people, and though it was not great, as we count greatness now, yet its existence was a proof of a worthy remnant in the midst of worldliness, that had not bowed the knee to Baal. Maryland and Virginia were excepted from its operations, because by the law in these colonies ample provision was supposed to be made for the support of the clergy. There were compensations, however, in favor of the other colonies; for the Society could exercise a scrutiny and supervision over those whom it acpected and sent out; which was the means of presenting the church in its truest and most acceptable form in those places where clerical shortcomings of any kind would have intensified the already active suspicion and dislike of the people. And so as a fact, though the church was dreaded, and was to the last regarded as the symbol and engine of ecclesiastical tyranny, and her ministers in times of strong agitation, were placed under the social ban ; yet there was an ever-increasing strength granted her by the gradual appreciation of her true principles. Nothing but a worthy body of high-toned Christian ministers could have secured this blessing.

In Maryland at this time, from 1722 to 1734, the condition of things was not pleasing. For the church was not in peace, and the occasions of disturbance were various. As to the outside bodies, her relations with them had in no way changed, and there was as much liberality towards all exercised in Maryland as any where else probably in the world. The Roman Catholic continued, of course, to stand in the same relations to society and the state in which he had always stood; while probably after 1715, when the family of the Lord Proprietary became protestant, and jurisdiction was restored to it, the strain was less than it had been before. The spirit of the English government towards Roman Catholics, was well exemplefied in its treatment of Lord Baltimore at the Revolution of 1688; for while withdrawing jurisdiction, which was felt to be unsafe in his hands, it secured to him all his rights of property in the colony, and when the family changed its faith, jurisdiction was restored. Its deprival of civil rights, however, did not affect, apparently, the numerical condition of that church, for it was able to preserve a constant ratio to the population down to the close of the colonial days, being about one-twelfth. Of course this was only kept up by a large immigration. The number of Jesuit missionaries, however, now in the colony, and they furnished the chief supply for the adherents of the Roman faith, was as large as it was at any subsequent time, as their official records show. For in the year 1723 there were at the Residence of St. Ignatius sixteen members of the society, twelve fathers and four coadjutors. The duty of the coadjutors, who were lay brothers, was to attend to the domestic affairs of the Residence, and to cultivate the land attached to it, the income from which supported the mission; while the fathers went hither and thither throughout the colony in the performance of their spiritual duties. This had been their rule from the foundation of the colony, and to obtain a certain and secured support had been the object of their large acquisition of land which early brought them into conflict with their patron. For there was no appointed income except this, other than the free-will offerings of the people; a fact that doubtless in certain localities gave them a great advantage at times when the matter of expense was a great subject of agitation. Not that it may have caused any persons to go over to the Jesuits, but it increased their opportunity to question and fault the ministers of the Established church, as now we find them doing. For in addition to other trials, the clergy were compelled to enter into public controversy in answer to the Romanist's bold challenge; to vindicate the truth of the Protestant faith against Romish perversion, as they had to vindicate the Establishment and their rights under it against the attacks of those, sometimes of their own household, who bore the Protestant name.

As regards the other great body of dissenters that had formerly given trouble, the Quakers, they by this time had ceased to excite much attention. They had come to be better understood everywhere, and the immunity they had almost always enjoyed in Maryland became more perfect. They had never been feared, but only regarded as extravagant enthusiasts, who, for certain matters of form, were ready to endure all things, and who despised the powers that be in so far as they interfered with their views and practises. But in Maryland things had been adjusted to suit their private notions of what was right; and as their lives as a body were peaceable and upright, and they were industrious, faithful,

God-fearing citizens, all possible liberty was willingly extended. And no anxiety seems to have been felt by the ecclesiastical authorities about their proselyting, as was felt about the Roman Catholic Church. It is true, in the beginning they had won over some persons from staunch church families, but this ceased, and they became a close corporation, living in themselves and to themselves. Thus they shut themselves off from sympathy; while even the persecution was wanting that first made them objects of observation. Also they differed from no other body of Christians on what would be esteemed great principles; for they were then orthodox in all the great matters of faith, believing in the Lord Jesus Christ for salvation. Since then they have marvelously changed. Their position as a dissenting body was that of the negation of rule, form, and ceremony; while the grand right of private judgement and individual responsibility, of which they had at first been eminent exponents, had come to be a part of the creed of all bodies; the English church, as we have seen, running to the very excess of that salutary principle. So the Friends in Maryland were now no longer feared. They were objects of consideration, but it was for missionary work. An attempt was made to send a missionary amongst them, and one of the tracts circulated was entitled "A Serious Call to ye Quakers," with probably, however, very little effect.

For the closeness of their body was rigidly maintained, and a thorough inculcation of their principles was from the earliest years a part of their children's education. They were taught that they were born in the "meeting" and that they were to esteem it a blessed birthright. Now and then, under the fascination of bright eyes or winning ways, a son or daughter would go off and be married by a "hireling" minister to one of the outside world, but such conduct was so strongly reprobated, with threats of prosecution and dire ill to the said hireling, that the offence was not likely to become common. The rigidness with which they maintained their separation is exemplified in their "Enquiries" of the year 1725, addressed to the members of the meeting, one of which was "Are all careful to keep up their ancient and Christian testimony against tithes, priest's wages, repairing of their houses, called churches, or any other ceremony of that nature." This their testimony was both ancient(!) and Christian(!) and as it affected not only their principles but their pockets, doubtless it was kept up. Thus they were brought into conscious antagonism with the great body of their fellow citizens, and as a fact they have always been a separated people in every society.

For their segregation went into everything. They worshipped apart, protesting, as we have seen, against the name of church; they married apart and banished every son or daughter who did not conform in this; their language, their views of certain social duties and obligations, as of oaths and bearing arms, were different; their dress even made them distinct from all about them. And the discipline of the meeting enforced and compelled these things. In all business matters, also, as far as possible, they kept themselves to themselves; one of the enquiries running. "Whether there are any masters of trade that want apprentices, or children of Friends to be put forth, that they apply themselves to the monthly meeting before they take those that are not Friends or put forth their children to such." Nor is this the only instance. Everything was to be done as far as possible within the society; disputes to be settled, the poor to be provided for and educated, and a general supervision to be exercised over various of the common matters of life. Afterwards thier views upon the then social institution of the country, slavery, separated them further from the people.

And this separation is probably the only cause why they have continued to exist. For as some among them believe now, who yet by old habit and education still retain their "birthright," Quakerism has seen its day of usefulness and now may without loss pass away. They have swung away from their old moorings in the matter of faith, and their ideas of spiritual enlightenment, and individual responsibility, and private judgment, of which in their earlier days, they were the most pronounced expression, have now become common property. One danger they avoided which with the other peculiarities is remarkable, because a danger that has destroyed so many other like societies, viz: the community of goods. A care for the general body and all its members was requisite, and a large submission of their will to the common voice; but with all the enthusiasm of earlier days, the rules of private thrift and individual wealth have never been forgotten, while the community has seldom been dishonored by sharp practices or the dishonesty of its members.

The church in Maryland was now passing through turbulent days, as extreme, probably, as any to which it was ever subjected. It had grown in numbers, the parishes in 1722 amounting to thirty-eight, with about three thousand communicants and eleven thousand families attached to it. The parishes also were well supplied, in 1732 the report being made to the Bishop of London that there was but one vacant parish in the colony. Indeed, from this time on Maryland was always well supplied with clergy, and that because of their independent position and the general sufficiency of the support provided. Towards the close of the colonial period there was even a superabundance of ministers in the province.

But with the general prosperity of the church there was also much misfortune, for as a fact this was a time of unusual discord. One of the occasions of this, manifest upon the surface, was the attempt to divide some of the parishes, a project to which the clergy showed their usual hostility, in which probably they were only too sensitive. For the parishes having been erected when the population of the colony was very sparse, many of them were exceedingly large, and far beyond the power of one man efficiently to care for; a stretch of territory sixty miles long and containing from four to five hundred families precluding frequent ministrations, and church services were necessarily denied to a large proportion of the people. But the attempt to divide excited the fears and the loud protests of

the clergy. They looked upon it as a blow aimed
at their interests, and an assault upon their
rights. They feared also the spirit that was
abroad, opposition to them being in the air,
and they looked out upon poverty and destitution as their oncoming portion. Even some of
the best men of the province had this feeling,
Mr. Wilkinson, the commissary of the Eastern
Shore and one universally commended, being
among the most earnest to protest. The civil
authorities, however, went forward, various
parishes were divided, and more laborers entered
the field, doubtless with exceedingly good
results.

The spirit that was abroad also manifested
itself in another way, and the fears of the clergy
were excited by an attempt to reduce the poll
tax by which their salaries were paid, the amount
of reduction proposed being one-fourth. This
was a sweeping measure bearing upon all the
ministers alike, and therefore it was apt to do
far more harm than the other; for while many of
the parishes might be too large, there were some
where the income was exceedingly small, and a
reduction of one-fourth meant distress and suffering to the minister. The agitation of this
question began about the year 1728, and, of
course, it excited the liveliest alarm. The clergy
sent up their protest and petition against what
they deemed an iniquitous measure; and truly
there was that about it which showed that the
authorities were not treating them sincerely.
For the plea was that over-production had
reduced the price of the staple, and the plan
proposed was to limit the growth and so force the

market up as that thirty pounds would be of as high a value as forty then were. But their want of sincerity was seen in the provision that the law allowed the planter to pay in money or tobacco as he might prefer, the rate of commutation being fixed, so that when the market was good the clergy would get money, but when it was poor they would get the tobacco.

Therefore there was good ground for alarm. For the law was passed by the Assembly, and the clergy in their extremity approached the society for the propagation of the Gospel for relief. They also by their agent, whom they sent to England, Mr. Henderson, approached the king, the proprietary, and the Bishop of London, seeking protection. As it happened the proprietary, with whom rested the power of vetoing bills passed by the Assembly, refused to confirm the law, and moreover, assured the clergy of his favor and protection. Probably, as it turned out, the agitation of this measure advanced their interests, as in 1729 a law was passed limiting the production of tobacco. In 1730, however, another measure was passed by the Assembly which allowed the payment of one-fourth of the tax in grain, which became a law. The clergy were at first alarmed, as they had been before, though experience of the measure seems to have removed their fears. Like many of the colonial laws it was enacted only for a given period, and was from time to time renewed. The condition of the clergy in the province was now, taken altogether, very much improved, for the population had in most parts greatly increased and their incomes were generally sufficient. In one parish, and that not an exceptional one, the taxables between 1698 and 1726 had increased about eighty per cent.

All this agitation, however was symptomatic, for the colony was in a turbulent condition, and as doubtless could not be avoided, the clergy were drawn into the prevailing disputes. Never had their character been higher, nor their conduct as men and ministers more commendable. Those in authority in the province testified to this. Many of them had long been residing in their parishes and their sympathies and their hopes were identified with those of their people. They were also, notwithstanding their diverse nationalities, more than one-half being English, nearly one-half Scotch, and the remainder Irish, generally harmonious among themselves, and met in convocation from year to year. Still when one came to describe them, as was done in 1722, a man might be said to be a good preacher, an excellent good man, a good scholar, or some less complimentary term might be used, but he was always a whig, a tory or a stickler for the present happy Establishment.

The occasion of this disturbance was a discussion that divided the colony for about ten years beginning with the year 1722: the subject being the extension of English statutes to civil and criminal procedure in the Maryland courts; one of those struggles that marked the spirit of the people and gradually prepared the way for the final effort for independence. According to the rule no statute passed by the Assembly was operative if disapproved by the proprietary, who under his charter had this authority; a power in his hands which the people feared would be prejudicial to their rights and liberties; and they also at this time claimed, what was a fact, that until now, when there was no colonial law covering a case, the courts had applied the English statutes. The upper house which always supported the prerogatives of the Proprietary, resisted this claim, and denied the fact; and the agitation became rancorous. The colonists insisted they were still Englishmen, and had sacrificed none of their privileges by passing over to the colonies; though they were inconsistent in this, that they accepted only such English laws as binding as were agreeable to themselves and found to be convenient; for they dreaded the prerogative of parliament as much as they did that of the proprietary. At that time, indeed, things were very much undefined in the whole matter of colonial administration; for England had not yet learned how to bring up her children. The question was finally settled with something like a compromise between the contending parties.

Into this agitation the clergy were almost of necessity drawn; for it was a subject that deeply concerned the interests of the people, the dispute arising upon the passage of an act in 1722 entitled "An Act of Limitation of Actions of Trespass and Ejectment." General principles were soon enunciated and the discussion spread everywhere. It is easy to imagine where the clergy would be found in this question; for born and reared as they almost all were, if not all, abroad, they had not that instinctive sense of popular rights which always characterized the American colonists, that jealousy of interference by any privileged person or class, so that now as always, the great body there were ranked upon the side of the proprietary and prerogative. This was almost inevitable; for prerogative was not an alarming word to them, it being their yearning desire all through the colonial days of Maryland to have the prerogatives of a bishop brought to bear upon their church life, and their strong conviction that such prerogative alone could save the church's fair name. This question was mingled with the agitation now. For it was just before this time that the attempt was made to secure from the Legislature the confirmation of the disciplinary power of the Bishop of London over the persons of the clergy, and it was during this agitation in 1727, that Mr. Colebatch, spoken of in the highest terms for his excellence was prevented by a writ of *Ne exeat*, issued by the colonial courts, from obeying the summons to go to England to be consecrated for the colonies. And so, in the personal abuse hurled by one of the leaders of the people at this time, Mr. Thomas Bordley, against commissary Henderson, he charges him with going to England to seek the episcopate.

The instincts of the clergy, therefore, lay with the proprietary during the struggle, and in a proportionate degree they were antagonized by the people. This was the assertion of Governor Calvert in 1726. They were opposed because they were supporters of the king and the proprietary. They were always on the side of prerogative, and doubtless it would be found, could the matter be fully known, that very much of the scandal that was uttered against them, had its origin in the jealousy and hatred born of political prejudice. For it requires but a very small foundation to enable animosity, so born to raise a very large and imposing structure. And so the agitation of the question about their salary, and the attempt to reduce the amount. It was as a punishment for their political opinions and the use of their influence against a popular movement.

But these were not the only means made use of to express the politicians' ill will. We have seen the attempt to divide parishes, for which in some instances there was some justification; but the antagonism showed itself also in raising the question whether the act of establishment had been duly passed, the same as was done in another great period of trouble. This, however, was not pushed, as doubtless it could not be. Another attempt was made to establish an ecclesiastical court for the trial of clergymen, to be composed in part of laymen; but this also failed, the Governor disapproving of the measure, both because lay jurisdiction was not sufficient in the case, and also because there was no call for such a court, the reputation of the clergy being good. Nor was it only by such public measures that antagonism was shown, but also the spirit that was abroad manifested itself in acts of personal violence, and blows were given, and sometimes returned by, the clergy. Even Gov. Calvert himself descended into the arena, though as it seems only to offer threats which he did not carry out. Mr. commissary Henderson, who stood forward for the clergy as their champion, and who was courageous enough to vindicate their position and their rights, came in for a very large share of the plentiful abuse. A tory of the tories, he was also both by temper and disposition, the man to be in the very thickest of the fight. If his enemies are to be believed, he was not wanting in the qualities of a practical diplomatist.

These troubles continued down to the year 1732, when the colony obtained peace by something like a compromise with the proprietary. Probably also the depressed financial condition, that had earlier been felt, had now been relieved by a better demand for tobacco; for the market for that staple has, it is likely, always been subject to rapid fluctuations, and with their increased resources the colonists had lost their irritation. Churchmen also doubtless had come to recognize the fact, that for them at least, the establishment afforded clerical ministrations at as small an exaction as any other system could provide, and they became content to let well enough alone; for for thirty years and more there was comparative peace.

The proprietary at this time was Charles VI, Lord Baltimore, a young man and new to affairs. He did not rank high amongst his contemporaries even in later years, for good judgment, committing indiscretions that have done more to immortalize him than his virtues have. Possibly his want of experience largely promoted the dissensions of the colony, though he showed a consistency and force during the great agitation, that indicate him to have been a man of force of character. He came into the colony in 1732, and the difficulties that had distracted the church so violently, particularly within the last two years since Mr. Henderson's return from England, were calmed down. For the clergy avowed themselves his strong supporters, and his kind feeling for them and the establishment, which had prompted him to stand their friend earlier in the contest, now made him their advocate and defender, assuring them of his protection. He also favored any attempts made by the commissary to execute the duties of his office in the exercise of discipline, though unfortunately his residence in the colony was so short that soon after his departure, Mr. Henderson gave up his commission in disgust, having been unable to accomplish any permanent good. With him the office ceased, as possessing but little authority or influence, and the clergy were left destitute of even a nominal head in Maryland. The authority of the proprietary under his charter and the law, could be exercised only to gall and irritate, while the jurisdiction of the Bishop of London, was for all purposes of administration, only a name.

It was at this time, about the year 1725, that the non-juring Bishops, Talbot and Welton, were in Maryland, where according to report, they exercised their office. They were, however, but coldly received; for they represented a party in the church which were bitterly opposed to the reigning family of Great Britain, and consequently they met with no sympathy in Maryland, where the clergy generally were loyal to the house of Hanover. And as also the laity of the province, as of America everywhere, were opposed to the Episcopal office, the work of these gentlemen was nothing. It has even recently been asserted, with abundant reason, that in the North one of the great leading causes of the American Revolution was the proposition to introduce Episcopacy; and certainly for years after that Revolution the office was looked upon with fear and suspicion. Maryland was no less sensitive than Massachusetts to the introduction of an irresponsible authority, and hence the failure of these non-jurors. The introduction of Bishops was strongly agitated at this time, and mention is made in 1724 of a legacy of two thousand pounds sterling, left by the late Archbishop of Canterbury, towards the support of a Bishop for the plantations. Perhaps, however, the most fortunate thing that could have happened to the church in the colonies, was the non-introduction of Bishops; for certainly had they been introduced with the privileges and prerogatives that go with the office, and with the associations that clung about it as an English institution, in the extreme suspicion and sensitiveness of the people to any approach to arbitrary power, the church would have lost many sons and daughters, and would herself have been put under the ban of public condemnation. For a Bishop hated and abhorred, would have been more damaging than many parsons scorned and maligned. A Divine Providence was doubtless ordering for the highest good.

CHAPTER XI.

THE PARISH.

The Rev. Peter Tustian, the second rector of St. James' Parish, took charge of the same on the twenty-ninth day of March in the year 1722. He had come to America in the year 1719, as a Missionary sent out by the Venerable Society, and had at first gone to South Carolina, where he remained but a short time, being found in St. Margaret's, Westminster Parish, Maryland, in 1721. The form of his induction runs as follows:

(Maryl'd S.) Charles Calvert Esq., Gov. of Maryl'd, Commander-in-Chief, to the Gent. of the Vestry of St. James's Church in Ann Arundell Co. Greeting:

Whereas, the Rev. Mr. Peter Tustian, an Orthodox Minister of the Church of England, was sent and recommended by the Lord Bishop of London and Diocesan of this province, to officiate as such in any part of America, I do therefore hereby recomend and appoint the said Peter Tustian to be rector of your parish, and direct you to receive him as incumbent thereof, and will you to be aiding and assisting to him in all things becoming, to the end he may receive the full bennifits and perquisites to his office appertaining, together with the forty pounds of tobacco per poll arising within the parish afores'd.

Given at the city of Annapolis this 29th day of March in the 7th year of ye dominion of the Rt. Honorable Charles, Lord Baron of Baltimore, Absolute Lord and Prop'ty of the province of Maryland and Avalon, &c.. Annoq: Dom. 1722, and in the 8th year of his Majesties reign.

CHA.' CALVERT.

For some reason this form of the induction of Mr. Tustian did not prove satisfactory to him, so that on the fourteenth day of July "he utterly disclaimed any benifits" arising from it, and presented a second letter bearing the date of the fifth of April, which reads as follows:

"By the Hon. Chas. Calvert Esq., Captain Generall, Lieut. Gov. &c., to the Gentle'm of the Vestry of St. James' Parrish in Ann Arund'll County. Greeting:

Whereas, the Rev. Mr. Peter Tustian has been sent and recomended by the Right Rev. Father in God, Jno. Lord Bishop of London and Diocesan of this Province, to officiate here as an Orthodox Minister of the Church of England, I do therefore hereby collate and appoint the said Peter Tustian, to be rector of your parish, and I do will and require you to be aiding and assisting to him the said Peter Tustian, so that he may have the full bennifits of the forty pounds of tobacco per poll arising within the parrish aforesaid, together with all other bennifits and perquisites thereunto belonging: Given, &c.

The two forms, it will be observed, differ in some respects, the second being in some particulars more explicit. There seems to have been no settled form at this time appointed, and it was probably to provide against contingencies that Mr. Tustian sought to have everything exact. He may have thought that difficulties might arise, as afterwards they did, between him and the vestry, and he would provide against technicalities upon which the vestry might seize. So that the Governor's title is more accurately given and the due legal name and style of the Bishop of London. Also, we have the term "collate" instead of "recommend," and the clerk's attestation is appended that such is a true copy. The times were beginning to get troublous, and Mr. Tustian may have proceeded out of abundant caution. The subsequent difficulty into which he got with the vestry proves him to have been a man of great persistency.

It will be observed also that both these forms differ from that of Mr. Hall in 1698, the reason of which was that in 1715, upon the Lords Baltimore becoming Protestant again, having abjured the Roman faith, the administration of their colony was restored to them, and continued in their hands till 1776. The Charles Calvert who who signed the above, was not the proprietary, as is seen, but of a collateral branch of the family. It is to be observed, however, that he acts by his own authority, and says "I collate and appoint;" for such was a governor's function under the law of 1702, it not being supposable, that while the colony was under the royal jurisdiction, the appointments to benefices in Maryland should proceed from a higher source. Afterwards when a coronet, and not a crown adorned the head of the absolute Lord of Maryland, the governors were, though long after this, deprived of this prerogative, and his Lordship, falling back upon his charter, collated the incumbents himself, a change in the agent that was not always profitable to the people. For the dignity of his Lordship's title was sometimes far superior to the dignity of his character, and boon companions of his revels in London, were the commissioned objects of his favor for Maryland.

Nor are we to understand of the Bishop of London's recommendation that it was any guarantee of the man's good character or qualification for ministeral work. For on a clergyman's presenting his papers, unless the Bishop knew of some error or fault in him he must receive him, and allow him to become eligible in his diocese to any position that might be bestowed upon him. He could proceed against him if he knew of occasion; otherwise the man was in good standing. That was all that was meant by the words of the induction, "sent and recommended." It would be sad to make a Bishop responsible for the bad men that may from time to time afflict his diocese; though it is to be feared that due scrutiny was not always used of the record of those sent over to America.

As regards Mr. Tustian, however, he was a good man, and at the same time a man of ability apparently. For in the year 1731, when the province was still in the throes of its great troubles, and also excited against the clergy in the matter of the forty pounds, we find him highly commended for having preached an excellent sermon before the Governor of the colony and the two houses of the Assembly, a good old custom of those days; for if there was some preaching to those honorable gentlemen now, doubtless prayers for them would be more effectual. His work in the parish also, would indicate that he belonged to a higher class of men. For fortunately we have two formal reports from him concerning the parish's condition. The first of these is in the year 1724, two years after he became rector, and from it we learn that there were then within its borders about one hundred and fifty families. Of these about two-thirds are described as attending church, while the dissenters are declared to have been, of Quakers forty families, of Papists five families, and of Presbyterians and Anabaptists one each. As many as forty persons sometimes received Holy Communion, which was administered monthly. The negro slaves are described as infidels, and their children but rarely baptised. Why this should have been so it is difficult to apprehend; because, as already seen, one of the difficulties that Mr. Hall had had in the beginning of his ministry, was because of his baptizing negro slaves. It may have been that Quaker influence, more than one-fourth of the people in the parish being of that name, or political misrepresentation about the civil effect of baptism, that it freed the slaves, or both, had caused the rite to be neglected. It is certain, however, as the register shows, that Mr. Tustian baptised very few of either whites or negroes, or if he did they are not recorded. One of the great leading subjects at this time was the care of slaves, and also of the Indians, some of which latter were still found in the province. Many of the clergy were diligent in baptizing the blacks, and Mr. Tustian, in his second report in 1731, says that he has in his parish large numbers of "christian negroes." And it was not only baptism that was insisted on; it was instruction as well. Upon this point dwelt the Bishop in his communications, and also the commissary; and often their appeals were responded to by not only the clergy, but by the masters and mistresses also. This is the testimony, while of course we find the masters, in some places, objecting to such instruction because it made the servants "rogues," a constituency of grumblers that existed to the last days of the "twin relic." A man of strong parts was ever able, however, to accomplish this, as all other good things. Mr. Tustian evidently possesed these parts, and certainly he took a deep interest in the slave; for in his last report made to convocation, he says, that "ever since he came into the the parish he had had a large number of Christian negroes." Some of them were communicants, and a great many had been baptised. The inconsistency between the two reports is probably to be explained by the fact, that at the time of the first one he was not familiar with the true state of things.

But it was not religious instruction only that was looked to and provided for. It was urged for all classes, the great work of the church in the midst of the unfavorable circumstances of the colony. But secular education was no less aimed at, a law having been passed in 1723 providing for the establishment of one school in each county, as near the centre as possible. The aim also was to make them free, and for that end a farm of one hundred acres of land was to be purchased. Certain fines also were appropriated in that way. How far the system proved effective is not known; though such schools continued to exist down through the colonial period. Some of them were afterwards combined together to form schools of a higher grade; for the course of instruction proposed for the earlier institutions, was not very thorough, the qualifications for the teacher being "That he be capable of teaching well the Grammar, good writing and mathematics, if such can conveniently be got." Charlotte Hall and Washington College had their origin in these schools. King William's School, out of which St. John's College grew, was instituted much earlier than this, being provided for by an act of the Assembly in 1696. These schools also were to be Christian institutions; and it is one item marking the esteem of the people and the confidence in which the clergy were held, that one of them was to be head of each county board of managers.

In addition to such schools there were various private ones throughout the colony, taught chiefly by the clergy, of whom there were many who were very well qualified for this task. For in all periods there were men of eminent talents and education, like Mr. Skippon, who in 1723 was described as an excellent scholar. They were found also able to wield a trenchant pen and whenever the battle of controversy raged they were found in the thickest of the fight. There were also schools sometimes on plantations, family schools with private tutors; though here the grade, one would suppose, was not so high, judging from the following advertisement under date of 1774, "To be sold, a schoolmaster, an indented servant, who has two years to serve. N. B.—He is sold for no fault, any more than we have done with him. He can learn book-keeping and is an excellent good scholar." Altogether, the standard of education was not generally high, and a great deal of what is called "quaint" as belonging to that day was simply odd because the work of the unlettered. But at the same time in all the departments of life, there were gentlemen of cultivation and learning, with extensive attainments; some of whom had gone abroad for their training; while the frequent agitation of the times brightened the wits and fostered the the consideration of great questions, so that some of the names of Maryland's worthies of that early period will never be forgotten. The planters, however, were doubtless not educated, but were blessed with abundant common sense and penetration; while the whole laboring class was ignorant of the commonest rudiments.

Some of the things mentioned in the records of those times surprise and interest us now, particularly because they are associated with some modern causes for discussion. Among these is the question propounded among the articles of enquiry of the year 1717 "Do your parishioners use due and lowly reverence when they hear the name of the Blessed Jesus"? Also "have you a font at the lower end of the church"? How they were answered we are not told, though probably the rules in such cases were observed in various places. If so, they had ceased to be, not only in

Maryland, but generally in other parts of America before the final disruption. There were, however, many irregular things done in those days, as we may well believe; for if discipline failed in other respects there certainly was not enough of it to keep men from indifference in the matter of rubrical order. Things were not as bad though in Maryland as they were in Virginia. For the picture which the Rev. Hugh Jones draws in 1724, though he had been in Maryland, was of things in the sister colony. Maryland churchmanship was always more orderly, chiefly because the pulpit was more independent of the pews, and consulted its own sense of what was right and becoming. Mr. Jones' words are: "In several respects the clergyman is obliged to omit or alter parts of the liturgy and deviate from the strict discipline to avoid giving offence. Thus surplices, disused there for a long time in most churches by bad examples, carelessness and indulgence, are now beginning to be brought into fashion, not without difficulty; and in some parishes, where the people have been used to receive the communion in their seats, a custom introduced for opportunity for such as were inclined to Presbytery, to receive the sacrament sitting; it is not so easy a matter to bring them to the Lord's table on their knees." The surplice was always used in Maryland, certainly in most places, through the days of the colony. In St. James' Parish this vestment is frequently mentioned, while there is no allusion whatever to the gown. How the great change could have come about that the gown became the vestment in common use, displacing the surplice, would afford a curious study.

St. James' Parish continued through all this period to increase in numbers and to grow strong in spiritual life ; nor is there any evidence that the skepticism that existed in certain parts of the colony was found here. How far it existed anywhere in the colony it is difficult to say ; for in this, as in a great many other things then, there was a good deal of exaggeration. Preachers preaching the truth were a great preservative against this pestilence ; and such blessing doubtless most of the parishes of Maryland, along with St. James,' enjoyed. That it did exist, however, the terrible law of 1723, before noted, indicates, a law like that of 1649, visiting with fine, forfeiture, branding, imprisonment and death any persons "blaspheming" the Holy Name, or denying the Trinity, or the Divinity of our Blessed Lord ; only the earlier act included under its ban those who should fail in reverence for the Virgin Mary. Whether such a law could have been enforced in the eighteenth century is doubtful, or whether it was only enacted as a protest by the civil authority against what was feared as a growing spirit of the times. Certainly the iniquity did abound abroad and was very fashionable. The law evidences one thing very clearly, that Christianity was felt to be the mainstay and hope of the province, and that offence offered to it was regarded as the highest crime. Maryland was not narrowly dogmatic, for all forms of belief and worship were tolerated ; but it was strongly religious and dreaded unbelief as an element and cause of ruin.

That St. James' continued to grow in numbers

is manifested by the further demand made at this time for the enlargement of the parish church. That demand was evidently very large and very pressing, and was satisfied in two ways; in 1722 a gallery being erected across the west end of the building, extending out ten feet, and in 1723 the east end of the church was opened and an addition of twelve feet made to it, thus together increasing the capacity of the church for worshippers much more than one-half, if not nearly doubling it. For outside the chancel in the original building there were probably not more than thirty feet available for pews. The contract for this last work sounds rather odd to our ears, being as follows: "Agreed with John Polston to build an addition to the east end of the church, extending twelve foot, and the same width of the said church, to be sealed within like the other part, to make a handsome altar-piece, a new communion table, two new window frames, and one for the end of the addition, if the vestry thinks convenient; to fix the bannisters around the said table, as before removed, the said Polston to find everything towards the said structure, having liberty to take framing stuff from the glebe land for the said addition; all which is to be done workmanlike; in consideration whereof the vestry agrees to give the said Polston nine thousand pounds of tobacco and liberty of making and disposing of the pews in the said addition, the said work to be done, &c." In due time the work was completed and "the said" Polston sold the eight pews, there appearing to be a very large demand; for as small as they necessarily were, the most of them were sold to two persons conjointly, and one of them to three. The era of church building had not yet set in, though from 1732 onwards churches were erected. The period of rebuilding came in later, about forty years after this time. The original small frame buildings had to do duty for some years yet. The distinction between communion table and altar is more in agreement with Methodist usage than our own at present, and like the present title, "Protestant Episcopal," found nearly sixty years before this time, shows that more things have been inherited from those days than we give them credit for. What may have been the architectural appearance of the church after all these changes, is a difficult question, but doubtless the longing was fostered for the time when a structure worthy of the parish and large enough to provide room for all that might come to worship, might be erected.

Things proceeded quietly in the parish during Mr. Tustian's ministry, the vestry attending to their various duties of caring for the material welfare of the church, the moral condition of the people, and the financial affairs of the commonwealth within their jurisdiction. The last they performed by appointing counters to regulate and control the growth of tobacco, the law forbidding at this time more than a limited amount to each taxable, 7,000 plants; with half that quantity to non-taxables. Their care for the morals of the people is shown by the following, of the date of 1733: "Upon complaint of Samuel Taylor and Ann Howard's unlawfully cohabiting together, this vestry has ordered that the said Samuel Taylor and Ann Howard be summoned to appear before them at the Parrish Church on Tuesday the 24th day of July, to answer to the above complaint." This summons was obeyed, and upon the appearance of the parties they were informed by the vestry that upon examination, the charge was well founded, and they were ordered to mend their ways. Fortunately such cases were now far less frequent. By a law passed in 1730, persons refusing to become vestrymen upon election, were fined a thousand pounds of tobacco, the amount at first laid upon church wardens for refusing to serve. If they did serve, the service was to be real and not merely nominal, for refusal or failure to attend the meetings of the vestry subjected the delinquent to a further penalty.

The church at this time came into possession of the silver bason which it still has, the gift provided for by the Rev. Mr. Hall in his will. In 1724 Mr. Tustian reported to the vestry that he had received from Mrs. Mary Hall bills of exchange for ten pounds sterling, which amount the vestry authorized him to expend according to the terms of the legacy, and in 1726 we have the account rendered for the total of the bason, ten pounds and six shillings. Also in 1723 we find William Loch Esq., informing the vestry "that it was the desire of his wife upon her death bedd to give the sum of ten pounds towards adorning the altar of St. James' Parrish Church with the Creed, Lord's Prayer and Ten Commandments, which according to her desire he is ready to comply with. Whereupon he desired the vestry to agree with the joyner for the same." This was done, and according to the lady's pious wish the tablets were set up, the same doubtless that at present are found in the church; having been transferred when the present edifice replaced the old one.

The last mention we have of Mr. Tustian as rector of St. James' was in the year 1732. In the year 1726 he had gone to England, remaining away probably over a year, as we have no mention of him for nearly eighteen months. Nor were any vestry meetings, it seems, held within this time except one, which may mean that the church was closed or that the rector's presence was needed to keep affairs active. After his withdrawal from the parish temporary supply was secured, apparently by the vestry, in the services of the Rev. John Urquhart, for nearly a year, and it is possible that Mr. Tustian made some such provision for his absence. The parish was peaceful during his incumbency, as far as we can discern, though the church in the province was so much disturbed. Later on, however, we find him engaged in a lawsuit concerning his salary, having sued the sheriff for sums due as Rector of St. James.' The vestry authorized the sheriff to allow the proceeding, and secured him against loss. The case having been passed upon in the colony and decided against Mr. Tustian, it was carried to England by appeal. How it was finally settled there we do not know, nor do we know what the ground of the suit was. It ran through a number of years, the appeal being taken in 1740.

CHAPTER XII.

THIRD RECTORSHIP.

GENERAL REVIEW.

The period we have now reached was, for a large part of it, marked with quietness both in England and the colonies. In the former the great series of whig administrations, which reached over an interval of about fifty years, persevered in their policy of peace, laying deep and strong that marvelous foundation on which England's glory and prosperity to this day rest. As before noted she sacrificed nothing in dignity by this policy; for she maintained always a position commanding the respect of the nations of Europe. How far her inactivity may have been the result of choice, or how far it may have resulted from the exigencies of her situation in respect of the house of Stuart, that through this period watched its opportunity to make a successful descent upon England, is a question; but certain it is that there was abundant opportunity for an active foreign policy in the wars upon the continent, had England desired such opportunity. Men of peace were, however, at the head of affairs, who loved peace for its fruits; and bending all their energies, and the force of a wonderful organization, to maintain their ends, they created a new England, both in the developement of home industries and in the extension of an all-embracing foreign commerce. Afterwards the country broke loose from her peaceful habits and entered upon a course of almost wild indulgence in foreign wars, and luxuriated in the sound of battles and the scenes of carnage. But whether peace or war, every policy advanced England's greatness; for to all quarters of the globe she at this time extended her arms and established the beginnings of the greatest empire that the world has ever seen. She lost America; for she had not yet learned how to keep her grown up children at home; and she would not recognize that the American colonies were not still in their nonage; but she gained much else in their place, and what she then gained she knows now how to keep, and she is the mother country beloved, admired, glorified, to millions in every division of the globe.

But these great conceptions had a secondary influence. For whether she regarded the ways of peace as advancing her internal prosperity, or whether as a giant she was struggling with the giants of the earth, so was her attention absorbed in the grander scenes that it became impossible for her to assume the narrowness of religious bigotry; but rather, by the very force of her circumstances her old persecuting edicts became practically obsolete and ready to vanish away. For bigotry and enterprise do not go hand in hand, but rather the former flourishes only in the self-absorption of a provincial temper; and to lift a nation or an individual out of this, and expand its faculties, its sympathies, its ambition, is the sure and efficient means of doing away with religious or social intolerance. So ancient Rome was tolerant of all religions until they were feared as working sedition. So Charles V. as in contrast with his son, was tolerant, though he lived in unfortunate days. So Holland, in the days of her greatness, was the freest of European states, and William III. of England, her pupil, the first liberal minded monarch of that realm. So the American colonies were in their earlier days intolerant in contrast to the times of their later expansion, when they were brought to contend for larger civil rights. Such narrowness in America died a hastened death because of the great questions that led to and were finally determined by the protracted struggles of the Revolution. Small objects become invisible as great ones loom up before the eye. And so the great comprehensive enterprise of the home country worked out its effects there. The national mind had no time for the old subjects that had agitated it.

To bring about this end had been the policy of whig ministries, a part of their general scheme for peace and quietness. The people must not be agitated, but every party and faction, as far as possible, conciliated. So with Walpole, who was the great leading figure of that period. His rule was, to offend nobody, but by every possible device to satisfy or keep quiet all. So with the Test and Corporation acts. Should he enforce these the whole body of non-conformists would be terribly excited, and Parliament itself would be shaken; but should he repeal them the churchmen, who had lost none of their sensitiveness, and the whole company of English squires, whose only learning then, whatever it may be now, was the traditions of their fathers, their prejudices and antipathies, would have been grievously offended. Neither of these things therefore did he do, but avoided danger for himself and his schemes, by allowing the laws to continue and having passed annually an act of indemnity for those who had rendered themselves liable to indictment.

This was the policy the Whigs pursued, and it has been more or less the policy of the Whig or Liberal party from that day to this,—to provide first of all for the things that advance the prosperity of the people at home. It is the party of advance and of constant adaptation, though when a vigorous foreign policy has been found necessary the liberal party has been found abundantly capable of prosecuting it. Speaking of this long continued Whig administration, an eminent authority of to-day, Green, in his Short History, says "Before the fifty years of their rule had passed Englishmen had forgotten that it was possible to persecute for differences of religion, or to put down the liberty of the press, or to tamper with the administration of justice, or to rule without a Parliament." Thus was laid the foundation of the England of to-day.

But this general delineation must be modified by a few other lines. For it is a necessary question, how far this liability of the government in regard to religious matters, was the result of statesmanship, and how far it was the result of indifference. It was doubtless the best possible rule to adopt, but also that time was in a remarkable degree distinguished for the scepticism of those highest in position, for depravity in morals and for looseness in the matter of social and domestic virtues. And all this was open and notorious, so that those highest in office as well as society, not only uttered the foulest language, but were guilty of drunkenness, and thought nothing of parading their excesses before the world. From the court down, the enormity was everywhere presented. There was not enough care for religion in high quarters to persecute because of it.

And the general rule held good, like people like priest, and that not only in the church but in the dissenting bodies. There was a decay of religion everywhere. England was striving to be rich, and wordly prosperity was abounding. Life, activity, enterprise, filled the land, and a great future was opening up before the minds of the people; and the inevitable result was that spiritual prosperity and eternity faded from the people's conciousness. They made no demand, had no interest in a pure, vigorous gospel, and the ministers of the gospel, hardly concious, may be, of the influences to which they were subjected, gave way before the deluge of the time. So that the testimony is the strongest possible that laxity ruled amongst the clergy as everywhere else. They were described as being "the most lifeless in Europe, the most remiss of their labors in private and the least severe in their lives." Nor is the testimony only by scoffers or by the wits of the ale houses. The clergy themselves are brought forward as witnesses; and the consequence is, that we must look back upon that time, the period which we have now under view, as presenting the saddest conceivable picture of apathy, indolence, self-indulgence, and recklessness of common report. The ale house, and the sporting field constrained the attention of those who wore the surplice; so that it was thought no disgrace to advertise: "Wanted, a curacy in a good sporting country where the duty is light and the neighborhood convivial." And public ministrations were in harmony with this, dull, cold, lifeless condition. Men were afraid, apparently, of showing interest in their work lest they should be reviled as "Methodists," and all were satisfied with the baldest presentation of heartless sentiments. It was from such persons at home that America had to be supplied.

But what else was to be expected? It was the day when the slave trade was promoted, when the knowledge of human rights was the lowest possible, when the Queen could issue her royal edict for the encouragement of the trade, when the protests of the colonists against the flood that was coming in on them, were regarded as little short of treason. A state of society where such things could be done, was not as yet capable of religious feeling of high order, or of response to generous sentiments. Religion is expansive and unless it expands it perishes. No man can love God as the God only of himself; he must love Him as the God of other people as well, as the God of all mankind. This was seen at that time, as in the burning heart of Wesley or of

Whitfield, who sought not only England but the colonies as the field of their labor. So all great religious movements have resulted in the extension of the gospel, and they have resulted either in the attempt to proselyte the people of the same country, which has often degenerated into persecution; or else the religious fervor has sought new fields wherein to manifest itself. So the England of that time. It had lost the disposition to proselyte the non-conformists, and its sense of the human rights of the heathen, was so low that missions to them were impossible. The nation that could carry on the slave trade could never so yearn for the souls of men as to send out Missionaries to preach the gospel. The trade was accompanied with the very extravagance of horrors. A voice of a Wilberforce that would not cease until it had made England sick with foul loathing of its own depravity, was necessary before England could rise up to the condition in religious matters worthy of the greatness God had bestowed upon her in the midst of the nations. A universal financial prosperity, a devotion to the business of the merchant and the chapman, had destroyed the power of apprehending better things, the things of God. The policy of Walpole, developed as Walpole developed it, was England's greatest bane. The heroic policy of which Pitt was the great exponent, though it drained the country of resources, and burdened it with a hopeless debt, proved infinitely more valuable for the true welfare of the country. Fortunately for England, and exhibiting the true merit of her people, forces were now preparing among the young men of Oxford, in the very midst of the spiritual barrenness there, whose operation was to renew the vigor of the cold lifeless body, and regenerate and energize all the strata of society from the highest to the lowest.

Now such being the condition of things in England, we should expect what we find, a measurable reproduction of the same in America. For the Rev. Thomas Bacon, writing in the year 1750 to the Venerable Society, dwells with great emphasis upon the very sad condition of things. Speaking of the prevalent scepticism of the day, he gives us some insight into the form it assumed by mentioning the influence of Tindal, who was a great light in the deistical world. Tindal called himself a "Christian Deist," choosing that title as best suited to the position he took in his most celebrated work, published in 1730, "Christianity as old as Creation or the Gospel a republication of the religion of nature." For the phase of his deism was, that claiming for Christianity the highest expression of a moral code and worthy of "an infinitely wise and good God," he denied to it all its claim to miracles. He was answered by such men as Dr. Waterland. He had, however, his day, and was received, because he was the expression of a certain morbid sentiment that at that time afflicted the community. For so without doubt are we to regard such passing states of society, whatever may be the cause. The moral and spiritual natures of men are afflicted with epidemics, as well as their physical frames, and the maladies of the one are as easily traceable to their causes as the other; while also the mystery that hangs about each of them is equal. As these epidemics return from time to time, it is a question for us now how far our period is afflicted or threatened.

But scepticism, in the great majority of cases, though by no means in all, is closely associated with, even as it has its origin in, a low standard of living, and itself promotes the growth of that which gives it life. And herein, doubtless, we have the prime occasion of many of the hard things that were said of the clergy through this time. Some of the clergy deserved, and some of them did not deserve, the reputation for dreadful things which was made to gather about them. A good man rebuking vice or reproving the wilful, gets scant justice from those whom he has endeavored to correct, and from all others who are in sympathy with them, and whose ways are frowned upon in the rebuke administered. Besides, if such persons have been able to become sceptics, as in reason they must desire, and if the times favor scepticism, as those times did, for it was in the air, the fashion of the day; then the rebuke is regarded as the insolence of of priest-craft, and woe betide the poor parson, every page of whose record is not written in clear letters of light for all to read. For if there be the slightest ground for a charge, or an apparent flaw on which to hang a misrepresentation, the whole body of sceptics is excited with apostolic ardor, and the whole company of God's ministers are made to suffer. Our Savior in His day was to some a glutton and a wine-bitter.

But not only in this way was evil wrought. The whole tone of the day was low. It was a time of transition, notably in America, and highly so in Maryland. People's minds were agitated by great questions, but they were all of the earth. And mixed with the questions were prejudice and bitter passions. Politics ruled the hour with all its demoralizing as well as its enobling influences, and finer sentiments were blunted. And the clergy, whose interests were involved in some measure, and whose instincts and education were in many ways played upon, sank to this level, and it became "like people like priest." They were secularized, they became worldly, they fell from the high position which by their calling belonged to them; and with this secularization they doubtless conformed to the world about them, until the better spirits among them looked on in grief and protested, but in vain. The Rev. Hugh Jones writing in 1741, tells us of this, and vainly looked about for a remedy. But remedy there was none. A Bishop could not be obtained, nor as we see now, would it have been for various reasons advisable. The commissary had surrendered his commission in disgust at his inefficiency; and as it happened, even what slight influence the Bishop of London had been able to exercise, was now cut off by the disagreement between him and the Proprietary. Bishop Gibson who had occupied that See for twenty-five years, dying in 1748, though in England his control was always felt in ecclesiastical affairs, yet for Maryland could do nothing. The Proprietary became more and more jealous of interference by any one in his colony, and the same jealousy was felt both by the clergy and the laity in their several spheres. For the former dreaded lay control, and the laity desired to retain all the liberty that they might possess.

The Establishment with all its great advantages for the time, had also its heavy drawbacks, and its vigor of action for good was always depressed. The church was in many things the victim of the peculiar circumstances of the day, both in its corporate aims and purposes, and in the condition of its children; and we are judging it now out of the happier circumstances of our time. It should have risen above its surroundings and vindicated in the midst of a naughty world its mission from its Lord. But alas! where is there one of us now that would like to have that judgment passed upon himself? for we are all victims of the day in which we exist.

As we have seen, the state of secular matters in Maryland always had a large influence upon the church, chiefly because all the great questions that agitated the colony grew out of the relations between the proprietary and the people, and that in such questions the sympathy of the clergy was far more apt to be on the side of the proprietary. They were generally the supporters of his prerogative. And this they were, not only because they were foreign born and educated, and because their church government involved the principle of prerogative, (though many among them from the Scotch universities were deeply tinctured with Presbyterianism, says one of that day); yet, doubtless, also, for the more evident reason that the proprietary, whose income was not affected by the forty pounds per poll, was more certain to be their friend, than the people who paid the tax. In some measure also the clergy were under the patronage of the Lord Baron, as they were given their cures by him or his deputy, and many were the kind speeches he made them from time to time.

We have seen the troubles to which the clergy were subjected previous to the year 1732 when peace was attained between his Lordship and the colonists ; and from that time the colony was in comparative quiet for several years. The church also enjoyed the benefit of this, and the records show less disturbance than, may be, at any other period during the Establishment. The truce lasted, however, only until the year 1739, when jealousy of the people for their rights as against the presumption of the proprietary, once more broke out. The question this time was not about the extension of English statutes, but about the proprietary's revenue, a matter that aroused as much interest and excitement as the other had done. Nor was it a question only of revenue, but of his lordship's rights to revenue ; the people showing a willingness to submit to an imposition, but insisting that it should be applied in a different manner. And this agitation lasted as long as the colony lasted, and was in fact very nearly allied to that which finally brought about the great disruption, the question of taxation by prerogative, and not by the laws of the people. The governor and council were able to thwart the will of the lower house, which had to content itself with occasional measures of reprisal and with the repeated passage of strong resolutions.

And what was the effect of this upon the church? The Establishment was not in any way threatened, as it had been in the earlier agitation, probably because it had been found too strongly established in the hearts of the people to justify at present a second attempt. But we find the old charges renewed against the clergy, and we find that loss of influence which is implied in the prevalence of infidelity and in the rise of new sects so strongly complained of. We also find the old feeling of antagonism renewed in the passage again of the act of 1730 affecting their salaries. This was done in 1747, and probably, nothing can show more strongly the condition of the clergy's minds with respect to the people, than the fact that they were quiescent in the face of this legislation, feeling doubtless that any agitation on their part would be without satisfactory result.

It was a time of radical disintegation; for the proprietary and his deputy in the colony, were the only ones that in any way exercised any control over the church. There was no commissary for the previous one had relinquished his office; the diocesan of the colonies did not utter a word, for it would have been, as to authority, but a sound; the proprietary was jealous of his rights, and maintained with consistency his control over ecclesiastical affairs, which the law and his charter gave him. Unfortunately, however, his character was not high, and though he could speak with kindness of the clergy, he could watch that in no way they should add to the difficulties that disturbed his province. In all things else their condition was satisfactory. Their income was abundant, and they were protected against any encroachment upon their rights and privileges. In fact the governor, through most of this period, Mr. Sam. Ogle, seems to have been well disposed towards the church and clergy, doing sometimes the unwonted thing of refusing to place in the care of parishes those whom he had reason to believe were unworthy. The form of his letter of induction, also, differing so materially from that of his predecessors, would indicate a certain prepossession in favor of the clergy, and a desire to do them all the honor possible, and maintain their rights in their cures. This form will hereafter be given. The clergy's income was generally ample, averaging in 1741, according to one of their own number, about two hundred pounds sterling. As many of them had glebes also, they could live in great comfort, for without land to supply a large part of the necessaries for the household, living was very expensive in Maryland. At this time, 1741, there were thirty-eight parishes or more in the colony, and the ministerial supply was generally abundant. Not all, however, were rectors, but some were called in only in emergencies or to serve during a temporary vacancy. In 1748 the population of the colony was reported as being ninety-four thousand whites and thirty-six thousand blacks. Some few of these last were communicants. As in 1722 the number of communicants was estimated at three thousand, the strong propability is that the church's comparative strength in 1748 was as great as it is at this time. What the increase was from 1722 to 1748 we do not know, but there is no reason why it should not have been equal relatively to the increase in population. Efforts doubtless still continued for the amelioration of the negro slaves, but as the slave trade constantly poured a great number into the colony, their improvement was as constantly retarded. Maryland always, however, felt her obligations to this class, and the influence of her orderly ways is still manifest in those who were formerly the servants of church people. From the present outlook, however, we can only fear, that for generations our power for more direct good is gone.

CHAPTER XIII.

THE PARISH.

The affairs of the parish throw some light upon the experience of the church in the colony at this time. The last mention of Mr. Tustian, as attending the meetings of the vestry, was on April 10th 1732, though evidently for some reason he regarded himself as rector until two years afterwards, and insisted, apparently, on receiving the income of the parish until his successor was inducted. The merits of his difficulty we do not know, nor the ground of his plea. We find, however, that he showed wonderful persistency, being convinced of the rightfulness of his cause; and that in carrying the case from court to court, and finally by appeal to England, he gave the vestry a great deal of trouble. The case was probably a notable one at the time. The vestry's counsel were Mr. Philip Key, Mr. Daniel Dulany, and Mr. Cumming. The Rev. Mr. Chase was security for Mr. Tustian, and in 1738 we find the vestry ordering that he be called on to meet the costs of the case, which, however, he refused to do. Mr. Tustian retained possession of parish property as long as possible, for in June 1734 we find the vestry ordering the church wardens to go to Mr. Henderson, his attorney in fact, and demand the surrender of the church library. Whether he prosecuted the case in England we do not know. The vestry immediately engaged a solicitor in London, but from some slight evidence it would appear that the case never came up.

Mr. Tustian's successor was the Rev. John Lang, a gentleman that had formerly been in Virginia, though he had now been in Maryland for some years, having preached the Visitation Sermon in Christ Church, Kent Island in 1730, being at that time rector of St. Luke's Parish, Queen Anne's County. As we can say of the two preceding rectors, he was a man of strong character, and commanded respect for his intelligence; while at the same time, as the records evidence, he was a man of amiability, and though afflicted with troubles, yet he loved peace and the quietness of his cure.

His letter of induction bears the date of May 24th 1731. One year of the two since Mr. Tustian disappeared from the parish, the church was ministered to by the Rev. John Urquhart, possibly engaged by the vestry, as they issued to him a certificate of service rendered. How it was provided for in spiritual matters during the other year we do not know. Mr. Lang's letter from the Governor is very peculiar, differing in some respects radically from the earlier forms. They had been addressed to the gentlemen of the vestry, who, however, were commanded to receive the bearer. This is directed to the minister himself, and reads thus:

Sam. Ogle Esq., Governor and Commander-in-

Chief in and over the province of Maryland, to the Rev. John Lang, sendeth greeting:

I do hereby constitute and appoint you to be rector of the Church of St. James in Ann Arundel County, to have, hold, and enjoy the said church together with all the rights, profits, and advantages whatsoever, appertaining to a minister of the said parish; and I do hereby require the church wardens, vestrymen, and all other the parishoners of the said parish, to receive, acknowledge, and assist you, the said John Lang, in all matters relating to the discharge of your function.

Given at Annapolis the twenty-fourth day of May in the twentieth year of his Lordship's dominion, Anno Domini, 1734.

Sam. Ogle,

J. Ross, Cl. Con.

What created this change in the form of the letter we cannot be certain of. It would appear that there was no set form up to this time but that it depended on the will or wisdom of the Governor for the time being. After the present occasion, however, we find this form used, not only by Gov. Ogle, but also by his successor Gov. Sharpe, and as but a short time before Lord Baltimore had been in the province, it is likely that the new letter was appointed by him. Another thing to be noted is that he does not mention the Bishop of London who was formerly recognized as sending clergy into the colonies, nor the king, the date of whose reign was formerly given. It is made plainly evident that it is his, the proprietary's act, by his deputy, and it is the assertion of his own independent prerogative.

This was his right under both the law and his charter. Also just before this he had passed through that long contention with the colonists about the extension of the English statutes to Maryland, a matter involving his rights and prerogatives over the people, and this letter was only, it is probable, incidental to and a symptom of his sensitiveness about his exclusive privileges. For as noted above, the letter is addressed to the minister, "I do hereby constitute and appoint you." and "I do hereby require the church wardens, vestrymen, and all other parishioners to receive, acknowledge and assist you." Claims could hardly have gone further, and want of consideration for the vestry could hardly have been more strongly expressed. Lord Baltimore was jealous of his prerogative, and afterwards he and the Bishop of London came to an open rupture, and the Bishop could accomplish nothing. Also he expressed himself strongly as the friend of the clergy, and he did indeed show a willingness to help them. How far his friendship was part of a scheme to maintain his authority we do not know, but we do know his private life proves that it was not the love of religion that made him the clergy's friend. Gov. Ogle who signed the letter, was a friend to the church, and sought to prevent evil men from entering upon the cure of souls. Nothing, however, indicates more clearly how widely removed we are from those days, how the feelings of the people and the spirit of our administration have changed. It is impossible for us to conceive of a vestry receiving at the hands of the secular power any one without question, whom it might choose to give a letter to, with order and command that they should extend to the bearer, not only his vested rights, but everything that might assist the functions of his office. But such was done then, and not only so, but the vestrymen were very earnest and faithful generally in the performance of their duties, submiting quietly as if the thing were exactly as it should be. They grew restive under this system after a few years, and sought to do their own appointing but for a long while they were faithful, attentive and laborious in performing their duties, equal in every way to many vestries under our freer and better order.

These days were not quiet ones in the parish, but for the first eight years of Mr. Lang's rectorship there was a good deal to irritate. We have seen Mr. Tustian's suit, and out of it grew another, which being with the rector in charge, must have created a good deal more feeling ; at one time the excitement being so strong that a vestryman refused to attend a meeting of the vestry in the parsonage, the rector being ill, when business of great moment was to be considered. The occasion of Mr. Lang's difficulty, was that at that time the vestry had a large amount of tobacco to its credit, which it was lending out, advertising for borrowers at the then legal rate of eight per cent.; and that Mr. Lang took over ten thousand pounds of this in the year 1735. The vestry generally required a heavy bond for double the amount of their loans, and well secured; but in Mr. Lang's case that was not given. Thus the matter ran on for some years until 1741, when the vestry made a formal demand for principal and interest, amounting in all to about fourteen thousand pounds. This Mr. Lang refused to pay, on the ground that he had become, at the request of the vestry as their agent, responsible in the suit of Mr. Tustian for costs, should the appeal go against the vestry in London; and also for any charges that might arise from the employment of the agent in London, which they had authorized him to do; and that he could not in justice be called on to pay the amount of their claim until there was reasonable certainty that he was not in danger from this cause. The vestry, however, did not admit the plea, and threatened suit, which apparently was instituted. In the mean time the trouble thickened. Mr. Dan. Dulany was Mr. Lang's counsel, and by his instruction, Mr. Lang refused to let the vestry have the key to the vestry house where the library was, which they were required by law to inspect; and also afterwards he refused them access to the vestry books they being in his possession. He also refused to attend vestry meetings. The case continued till October, 1742, when we have the following interlocutory judgment: By the Governor and council, 7th October, 1742.

Vestry of St. James parish:—Upon considering the petition and answer and what has been alleged on each side; this board judging that some other expedient than a decision on the point in question might be more likely to reconcile the incumbent and vestry; they for that purpose think proper to recommend to the vestry, as it is really a matter of justice and compassion, to make Mr. Lang a reasonable satisfaction for what he has expended, or is liable to pay, on account of any such buildings and improvements as he has made on the glebe, and which might be necessary and convenient for the incumbent to have; Mr. Lang giving sufficient security to indemnify the vestry for any tobaccos allowed him, and that whatever tobacco (if any) Mr. Lang has actually received from the vestry out of the tobacco in dispute to be deemed a part of what shall be allowed to him.

JOHN ROSS, Clerk.

Mr. Lang accepted this judgment for his part, and on Sunday gave notice to the vestry to meet him the following day. This they did, and in due time a settlement was finally reached which seems to have been satisfactory to all parties. The course of the proceeding seems to have been, first a prosecution of Mr. Lang for the amount of tobacco loaned him, and then a counter suit by him for improvements made upon the glebe. The agreement at last reached, carried both points, and ever afterwards Mr. Lang's residence was spent in peace. His first plea about his liabilities in their behalf in London seems to have been withdrawn.

The large amount of tobacco the vestry were handling at this time, was probably the accumulation of the years of the interregnum after the withdrawal of Mr. Tustian. For by the law the tax was always collected, and the amount, when there was no demand for it to pay the incumbent, was to be used by the vestry for the building and repairing of churches and the buying and stocking of glebes. In 1740 one person stood indebted to the parish for forty-five thousand pounds.

It is certain that already before this time the rectory had been built, though not many years before, as Mr. Tustian had reported that there was no house on the glebe. Mr. Lang's use of the money that came into his hand was evidently for a legitimate object, though he had not the authority to so apply it. The currency, while it lasted, was a great burden to the vestry, being difficult of recovery when loaned out. What finally became of it is not known. What surprises us is, that even with this large amount on hand the vestry from year to year petitioned for various sums for defraying the current expenses of the church, and their petition was granted. The vestry were the more reckless about suits probably because they personally were protected, and even their private expenses paid while attending upon the cases. The governor and council, often having had their attention drawn to the matter, as above seen, evidently felt that there was need of an examination, and so ordered the vestry of St. James' to return to them the amount of assessments and other sums received within the last ten years since 1732. This they had a right to do, and evidently at times there was need of such scrutiny. The vestry immediately required their register to make out such an account and forward it.

How far the offertory was observed in those days we are not told, though there can be scarcely a doubt that the offering on Communion Sunday was the only one made. That there was one then is evident from the fact that the alms bason was presented by Mr. Hall for "ye perpetuall use." No demands were made on the people except by the sheriff. Private gifts were, however, made; for at this time, as was done in the previous period, we find a gift of a handsome baptismal bowl provided for as a legacy. Another source of revenue was the fines laid on absent vestrymen, though these were not very numerous. The amount in each case was one hundred pounds of tobacco, recoverable in the County Court. Altogether the tone does not seem to have been so high as it had been, either because of the jarrings of the time and the restiveness of the people against Lord Baltimore's high assumptions, or because of the parish difficulties and irritation against their pastors. Mr. Lang was a man of peace and sought "to prevent future janglings and disputes" by a measure of conciliation. Also he was not a self-seeking man, as he was desirious of renting "Wrighton" on terms that would cut him off from all revenue, proposing that it should be rented for twenty-one years for the consideration that certain improvements should be made upon it. This was not accepted by the vestry, who required an immediate revenue.

But the authorities of the parish had not only tobacco to manage, and to turn over their capital from year to year at a heavy rate of interest; though in 1742 the rate was reduced one-half. They were a vestry for other things as well, for we find them at their old functions of endeavoring to restrain the immoral and to preserve the proprieties of life in the parish. The sin which was at one time common, when children, the fruit of unlawful miscegenation, were with both parents, the negro and the white, sold into slavery, seems now to have been abated, the lowest classes apparently being lifted above that degree of degradation. There was, however, much cohabiting, and the vestry had occasion frequently to sit as a court for the trial of such persons. Their power did not extend beyond the admonishing of the culprits to separate. On one occasion we find them demanding of a man that he come forward and show his marriage certificate, and once we find the husband complaining of the bad conduct of his wife and her unlawful relations with some one else. In this way the vestry became a threat to evil doers, and doubtless in a large degree very often restrained men from open sin. The church also was regarded as the law's bulwark against a certain class of misdemeanors; for according to the law of 1723 not only was the minister compelled to read the ordinance against blasphemy, swearing, sabbath breaking, drunkenness and selling liquor on Sunday, but the swearing became a misdemeanor when it was done in the presence of a vestryman, church warden, and other persons named. It is to be hoped that the vestrymen and wardens were always so circumspect as not to render themselves liable to whipping post or stocks by swearing in their own presence. This was the punishment meted out, the offender not being a reputable person. In 1747 the vestry had both those instruments of shame and pain erected, evidently, near or at the church, for the order for them is given, without mention of places, along with an order for a church door, seats in the porch and church yard, and horse blocks. They were evidently regarded as a convenient and helpful provision for church discipline. We see later how on one occasion they were used.

The vestry of course had the power of protecting the congregation in the time of worship, a power we find them exercising January 4th 1737 when the following order was passed:

"Whereas, sundry persons in the time of Divine service make a constant practice of running in and out of the church to the fire in the vestry house, to the great disturbance of the rest of the congregation; for prevention whereof for the future this vestry have ordered the sexton that before he tolls the bell he lock the vestry house door, and desire all persons to go out; and if any person refuse the sexton is ordered immediately to acquaint the church wardens therewith, who are ordered to do their duty by requiring all disorderly persons either to better behave themselves or depart from the church." This, it will be observed, was passed in mid-winter, and the reason why persons were so keenly anxious to go to the vestry house was, that there was no fire in the church, while a great glorious fire was roaring itself away in the vestry house chimney. They had evidently a keen regard to the proprieties of the house of God, and would not have the hour of worship disturbed. They were evidently a sturdy race, look at them as we will, whether as to religious earnestness or to physical endurance. There are a good many congregations now for whom it would be well if those old men could come forward and prescribe.

But it was not only in mid-winter they had trouble. We find in June 1747, a kindred evil harassing their patient souls, and again we see the wardens, as officers of the peace, ordered to do their duty. This order was passed at that time: "That the church wardens do prevent the negroes from going in among the white people to disturb them, as frequently they have done, and to prevent their going in and out of the church in time of Divine service, as they often make a practice of it." This is interesting as showing the colored people less under restraint than we could well have imagined them to be. They were at church and attended Divine service, but as they are to this day, they found themselves unable to sit still. And not only in church, but outside also, we find them moving about freely, going in and out among the white people, their masters, who were standing or sitting about in the church yard. Evidently also it was not one or two who did this, or only occasionally, for that would hardly have called for the vestry's action; nor were they moving about as servants to obey some order; but it was of their own free will, in numbers, frequently. This is an unexpected picture of old Maryland life, a degree of simplicity that we do not find now. For first the negro seldom or never comes to the white man's church, but has, because there only he feels free, a church of his own. Or if he should come, he would not be found moving about among the whites, but the few present would be off in a place to themselves, or perched upon the church fence; and they would file into the church after the white people were in. The relations of servant and master then were evidently not very rigid and stern; and while subserviency was demanded, and every order was necessarily obeyed, the relation was rather patriarchal. There were communicants of the church among the people of that race throughout all that period and ever since. In fact the kindly feelings that are still mutually entertained between the negro and the white man, bespeak the generous relations in Maryland of that institution.

But while the vestry possessed such functions, and were thus a power in the land in many ways for good, and doubtless at that time, of very great value for the moral welfare of the community, they were not allowed to feel themselves above authority in anything, but were required to recognize the administrative officers of the province. Thus we have seen how on more than one occasion they were called on to return an account of revenue received and how it was disbursed. On another occasion we find them compelled to apply for authority from the Assembly to lease a given piece of property, called Wrighton. This was a legacy to the parish for the benefit of the minister, and it seems always from its great remoteness from the church, to have yielded but a small revenue. Afterwards it was very much neglected, so that in 1744 it seems to have been destitute of many necessary things. The Assembly passed an act empowering the vestry to lease for twenty-one years, and Mr. Lang, the incumbent, showed his generosity in proposing terms that would ultimately benefit the parish minister, but be of no immediate good to him, and probably never of any benefit.

Why an application for an act of Assembly should have been made, is not evident; for the property had come to the vestry without other condition than that it was for the use of the minister of the parish, and apparently they would have the ability to rent it in any way or any terms they might think proper. It may be that the vestry of St. James' found itself not entirely trusted, and so feared to act on its own judgement. This one thing, however, is evident, the interests of the clergy were looked to notwithstanding the wrangling of the times. Their standing in every way in Maryland was one of independence and honor; their position was impregnable and their interests in every way duly cared for. The second clause of Mr. Terrett's will, dated 1693, reads as follows: "I give and bequeath unto my son, Nicholas Terrett, my great Bible and two negro slaves, to be between fifteen and thirty years of age, to be delivered when he becomes of age." The old gentlemen had very evidently a clear apprehension of what constituted the wealth of both worlds, though some would now say that he did not discern so clearly the due proportion of things when he transferred to his son the covenant of his own freedom and the bond of his fellowman's slavery. But these are modern notions, and the world then from the beginning had believed the old gentleman to be right.

To scan the church at this time, 1748, would in no way afflict one with pain; though it is true that the early glow of affection and devotion for it would seem to have paled somewhat; for the gifts that had at one time been frequent, seem now to have ceased. The church had gotten into a groove, and working as an institution, and the spontaneousness of early relations had ceased. There had been too much discussion about salaries, too much agitation of the forty pounds poll, a question that was at this time affecting the minds of the people. The clergy had had too much to do in the battling for what they esteemed their own. The church, also, as represented by the clergy, had been too much recognized as a distinct power in matters political, and that not in harmony with the great will and growing convictions of the people. Consequently spontaneousness had ceased as an expression of church life; but on the other hand regularity and order were eminent. The church was duly cared for in every way. The officers were required to do their duty. The building was kept in the best possible condition and the proprieties duly observed during holy worship. The ordinances were regularly administered and the young people as they reached the years of discretion, were admitted to the Holy Communion. Sufficient authority was committed to the vestries to make them diligent, and the many diffierent offices they had to perform in their two-fold capacity of church and civil officers, constrained their attention. Also the requirement of the law that they should meet at a given time every month with or without notice from the minister, though it is true the law does not seem always to have been faithfully observed, saved the parish from that indifference and neglect that is the sole cause of the poverty of so many parishes of Maryland to day. For in many places the vestry meets but once a year, at Easter, and frequently to perform only certain routine duties. But such was not the case then, but eight good men, vestry and wardens, were compelled, under penalty, to meet, and talk, and think over church matters, and the law provided sufficient funds for every purpose. Therefore, though the earlier youthfulness was gone, order, regularity and propriety were in all ways fostered. That, with a sound gospel preached, as doubtless it was, in the forty or fifty pulpits of the colony; and with the worthy lives of the clergy, (as the great body were worthy), who went in and out among the people, gave to Maryland religion a character which no voluntary organization could have done.

Mr. Lang ended his ministry the twenty-sixth of September, 1748, having been rector of the parish fourteen years, not an unusual length of time in those days; for then there was no getting rid of a minister if he wanted to stay; while for him the facilities for change did not exist, the whole matter being determined by one man, the Governor. Besides, St. James was a good parish in the light of its revenue, as doubtless in every other light; for in 1748 there were one thousand taxables, which at forty pounds per poll would have yielded at least eight hundred dollars. This with the two glebes, was all that was necessary for comfort, even with the high price of everything that was imported. The people soon felt the loss of their regular church ministrations, and November 1st petitioned the Governor for a successor to Mr. Lang. This was answered February 23rd of the following year by the presentation of Mr. Charles Lake to the rectorship.

An inspection of the library at this time

showed that some of the books were missing, having been loaned out to persons in the parish. The following plate and other articles were delivered up by Mrs. Lang: "One silver flaggon, one silver cup, one silver dish, and one silver salver, two surplices, one Damask table cloth, and one Damask napkin," and it was "ordered that William Journey, sexton, carry the above plate and linnen to Mr. Nath. Dare, Church-warden, to take care of the same, and that Mr. Lewis Lewin, one of the vestrymen, go along with him to see it delivered." That is the way things were done. Also, at this time we read: "Oct. 4th 1748, came before me, the subscriber, one of his Lordship's Justices of the Provincial Court of Maryland, the several persons under-noted, being all vestrymen and church wardens of St. James' Parish, and took the oath on the Holy Evangely of Almighty God according to the directions of the act of Assembly passed in the year 1748, in order to qualify them for the choice of the inspectors in the sd parish."

JOHN DARNALL.

We may not like the flavor of the times, but it is only because we have been fed on diffierent diet.

CHAPTER XIV.

THE FOURTH RECTORSHIP.

The period to which we have come, the fourth rectorship of the parish of St. James, beginning with the year 1749, and reaching to 1763, was in many respects one of great activity, not so much in ecclesiastical matters indeed, as in civil concerns, both in the colonies and in Europe. How closely, however, ecclesiastical and civil concerns were united at this time, how much stronger a hold the church had upon men's minds and filled their thoughts, then than now, is evidenced in the great seven years' war that began in 1755. For during that struggle, which had no more to do with religion than the more recent wars between Prussia and Austria, or Prussia and France, prayers were offered up here in America for Frederick as the great champion of Protestant Christendom; while the Pope celebrated Austrian victories as upholding the great cause of his church. It was indeed a great contest between Protestant and Roman civilizations, an expression of the inherent antagonism which the two systems embodied, a reproduction, after more than a hundred years, of what had been expressed with so much greater vividness in the thirty year's war. But Frederick of Prussia was not one to expend the resources of his dominions in defence of Christianity. He was not a second Gustavus Adolphus. Nor was England at all at that time enthusiastic for the faith. Nor on the parties on the other side can a higher eulogium be passed. It was something far nearer to their present interests that moved them, the glory and dominion of this world. Still the great struggle was made to wear that aspect of religion, and for both parties prayers ascended to heaven from those whose minds were deeply impregnated with the thought of the great cause.

Associated with this war in Europe was the French war waged by the colonies in America, a war that was momentous in its influences upon the future of the colonies; for it was by the fruits of it and the destruction of the French power in America, that the colonies, being rid of this threatening neighbor, were enabled to assume such a pronounced position towards the mother country. It will be remembered that this position was assumed very soon after the close of the French war in the discussions that preceded, and the vigorous measures that followed the passage of the stamp act. The whole period, however, was full of jealousy, the colonists always proceeding as far as they dared in antagonizing the will of the home administration. Nor was the jealousy only on the one side, for there was constant fear of the colonies as well, and everything was avoided that could in any way foster the spirit of independence. In this temper we find the mother country acting when Secker,

Archbishop of Canterbury, who was translated to that see in 1758, attempted to send out bishops to the colonies. It is true a large part of the opposition is attributable to the very low estimate that was made of the clerical office and even of episcopal dignity. For the episcopate had come to be regarded as merely a means of rewarding some minister whose services had pleased or been useful to the state. The grand thought of its true functions before Christ Jesus, was lost sight of. But Archbishop Secker's attempt was reprobated in the strongest terms. The clergy for America must be sent from England, America must be kept in this way, as in all others, dependent. So there was an "enormous outcry." One bishop declared "that the authors of this attempt ought to be covered with contrition and confusion"; and an archdeacon described it "as a mere empty chimerical vision, which deserves not the least regard." The matter, therefore, as so many times before, came to nought. Unfortunately there was nearly as much opposition to the scheme in all parts of America as there was in England. For if England dreaded to have the colonies independent in anything, the colonies equally dreaded to have an institution set up such as they knew the English episcopate then to be, and such as tradition had represented it, without practical force for the church's good, and and yet endowed with extensive prerogatives. America, therefore, continued to be dependent, but the only effect was, that, not having a native clergy, the ministers had no weight with the people in the great measures and ideas that were more and more engrossing the popular mind; and when the time came for acting they were casted off as having no living connection with the body politic. In the meanwhile they were on all sides suspected and subjected often to harsh treatment.

Along with the French war there are various things brought to the surface in Maryland that are at any rate interesting and that throw light upon the life of those times. It was begun in America before it began in Europe, and in 1754, Maryland, by a supply bill, made provision for her share of the expenses. Again, in 1756, she attempted the same, but as it happened she did nothing, not because she was not willing, but because of that inherent jealousy on the part of the people, as represented in the lower house of the Assembly, against the pretensions of the Governor and the upper house. As there was no great urgency, and as neither party could lose by the struggle, there was the greater willingness to keep up the contest.

One of the matters was the question of taxing convicts brought into the colony. For, most unfortunately, for many years there were very many of these brought in, at the rate of four to six hundred annually, a terrible class to turn loose upon a community, as jeopardizing both life and property, and having a most baneful influence upon the morals of the people. Though as the gallows were in such constant demand in England, it was hardly as bad as we should find it now. The proprietary claimed the right to tax this class of immigrants, the tax being laid on those that brought them over; while the lower house claimed the right to tax as their prerogative, asserting that such came under the head of servants, and that they had always, from the days when Maryland was a royal province, exercised this right. We have seen this when they taxed Irish servants coming in, "to prevent the growth of Papacy." The revenue to be by this means received, was to provide a sinking fund to meet the supply bill. With such a class precipitated upon the colony in spite of frequent and bitter protest, we cannot be surprised at the severe laws that were sometimes passed. It was estimated that from 1715 to 1763 there were from fifteen to twenty thousand such persons brought into the province. It is to be said that some of these were sent over for very slight offences; and that among them Maryland received some of her most skillful artisans. elegant mansions in and around Annapolis having been built or adorned by their hands.

Another matter connected with the supply bill and the tax levied to provide for it, though this bill was never passed, was the amount to be laid upon non-jurors or Papists. This item shows the animus of the times, and that very much of the old feeling against the members of this church still continued. As we have seen, the the war that was raging in Europe, the fringes of of whose strife touched America, and were the cause of the supply bill being called for, wore in the minds of many, a semi-religious aspect, both Pope and Protestant praying for the respective sides. This may have been in some measure the cause of the proposed legislation against the members of the Roman Communion, though it is also said that ill will for certain favorites of the proprietary influenced the minds of the members of the lower house. It is hardly possible, however, that so large a section of the people should have been treated so unjustly merely to gratify a little private animosity. The Roman church was still an object of dread and of dislike, and because certain members enjoyed positions of honor or emolument the general feeling of antagonism was very strongly expressed.

The proposed law discriminated against the Roman Catholic so far as to lay a double tax upon him, and as the tax was a very general one, covering all species of property, real, personal and mixed, all debts, and all imported merchandise, together with incomes, and as the Roman Catholics were about one-twelfth of the people and many of them were exceedingly wealthy, the intended burden would be very great. A vast amount of the old leaven was still amongst the people, and the principles of toleration were still unknown. Nor was this merely a passing fit of spleen; for the bill was passed by the Lower House at nine different sessions, showing a set purpose. But it never became a law, the Upper House rejecting the bill every time. They were called non-jurors because they would not take the oaths necessary for enjoying the rights of citizenship. They enjoyed privately the right of worship and protection; but as yet they were not emancipated, and were looked upon as not being safe as citizens. The oaths at this time exacted were exceedingly severe, as we shall hereafter see.

Another item, provided for in the first supply bill, is worthy of a passing notice, especially as it was associated with the duties of vestries.

We have seen the intention of the law makers, that it was to tax everybody and everything, and it would seem that they did reach everything that could readily be named. One item, however, surprises us even in their list, and that is bachelors, for we can not see why a man should be taxed for everything he has and then in addition by a special provision for that which he has not, the best of all possessions, a wife. Nor was it exactly a poll tax, for it was rated according to income and age, those under twenty-five years being exempt, and also those whose income did not amount to one hundred pounds per annum. Above that age a bachelor whose income was one hundred pounds, had to pay five shillings and one with an income of three hundred pounds had to pay one pound. Whether also it was regarded as a repressive measure we do not know, a nuisance to be abated. But that seems hardly likely, as it was immediately associated in the category with wines, liquors, and billiard tables; by what law of association we cannot say, though possibly the law makers could. Of course the bachelors paid the tax without protest, which is not what the Roman Catholics did, for they protested very loudly against the proposed unequal tax upon them. If the intention of the law was to make men marry it was not always successful by any means, as the lists returned by the vestries, who were the returning board for this purpose, show that some bachelors went through the whole eight years the tax was collected. The tyrannical law of the legislators could not deprive them of their liberty.

The law, however, was not so incongruous to

them as it to us, for we find a law advocated in England in the time of William III. for the relief of his Majesty, by which a tax was proposed on "marriages, births and burials, and upon bachelors and widowers for the term of five years," so that by it whether you lived or died, married or remained single, preserved your blessing of a wife or were utterly bereaved, the law would reach you. The Maryland proposition was merciful beside that. It only taxed bachelors along with wines, liquors and billiard tables.

Among the other immigrants received at this time into Maryland, differing from those they found there, in race, language and religion, were the Canadian French from Acadia. They came involuntarily of course, the English having, in the beginning of the French war in 1755 pursued towards them a most cruel policy. For refusing to take the oath of allegiance to the king upon the British occupation of their territory they were compelled to abandon their pleasant homesteads, which were given up to the flames; and taking what little was permitted them on shipboard, to be scattered everywhere. Some of them even reached Louisiana, while the most of them found refuge in the English colonies. Maryland received some who settled within the present limits of Baltimore. Longfellow in Evangeline has given immortality to this dark and cruel episode of war.

Looking more narrowly at the church affairs of Maryland at this time we do not find things wearing an attractive appearance, but rather it was a period of vexation and difficulty. And first of all we find a man possessing the privileges of the proprietorship of the province, Frederick, the seventh Lord Baltimore, who in nothing attracts favor, being ignorant, conceited, and with an overweening sense of his own prerogatives. Besides, when he succeeded his father in 1751, he was young, being only twenty years of age. He esteemed himself learned, and thought God had given him too much genius, expressing a wish that his Creator had bestowed less mind and more bodily vigor. In addition to these unfortunate qualities he was very immoral, having companionship with some of the vilest of the land. He was arraigned as a criminal in a very extreme case of wickedness and was commonly believed to be guilty. It was the misfortune of the church that such a man fell upon times when the colony was agitated by great questions, and when the matter of right and prerogative was uppermost. Because of his character, therefore, and the authority he wielded over the church, the better relations that existed between the Bishop of London and himself produced very little profit to the church.

Nor were all things favorable in the church itself. First of all there was a very numerous body of dissenters, Quakers, Presbyterians, Roman Catholics, Baptists, Dunkers, Lutherans, and doubtless others, who by this time had become powerful; and who, with the exception of the Roman Catholics, as voters were able to wield a large influence. These all of course opposed the establishment, looking upon the compulsion on them to support it as being an outrage. The largest two of these bodies had ever kept up an unvarying protest. Associated with these in the same cause were all those who were skeptical in their views or reckless in their lives ; which was also a large class. So that the establishment had many enemies ; and that it stood the pressure as it did shows how numerous its friends were.

Unfortunately also the circumstances of the church were rather helpful to the malcontents ; for there were some men, though, doubtless, relatively, but few in number, who were dishonoring their calling as ministers and exposing the cause to gross misrepresentation. Governor Sharpe tells us of one who "with great difficulty escaped the fate of a murderer, who received his thirty pounds poll while in prison." The rule, *ex uno disce omnes*, however, does not apply, for beyond all others the clergy were most earnest to have these things corrected. Besides, instances of shame in all bodies now are too numreous to enable us to compare ratios with certainty with the men of that day.

But something that is tangible is given us in the statement of Governor Sharpe that the colony and the church then were beset with clergymen from the Scotch universities, and that the cry went up that nearly one-half the people were "preached to in an unknown tongue." It will be remembered that this was not the first time that such complaint was made. Mr. Wilkinson, the commissary for the Eastern shore, as early as 1718 had written that they did not want any more of the Scotch clergy, because they were "young, raw, undisciplined, tainted with Presbyterian principles, and not real friends to Episcopal government." And though doubtless some of the charges against them were exaggerated, yet the good broad Scotch accent in which they rejoiced, together with the abundant antipathy of race and kingdom which was prevalent a hundred years ago, made them unfit for the English parishes in America; for such the colonial parishes were. There could not be much attractiveness in the church, nor much enthusiasm for it, in the nearly one-half of the parishes where these gentlemen were found.

But there was a deeper cause than this at work. The system itself was wearing out, the Establishment was becoming out of harmony with the times. American sentiment was growing very rapidly, and that sentiment meant absolute equality both as to person and property, before the law; and of this equality the Establishment was a curtailment. Other disturbances were rather symptons of this deeper disease; objections were strongly expressed because there was a more or less conscious antagonism to the institution itself.

This growing instability of the Establishment was perceived by some of the clergy, who during the frequent discusions upon the matter of the clerical salaries, were more apprehensive for the existence of the law of 1702 than they were about their incomes. For the readiness and the facility with which the Assembly tampered with one section of the law, made them fear that the law itself might become a common thing in handling, and at last without consideration be cast aside. And doubtless there was good reason for just that fear. Also, as the records show, there was more than one occasion when the validity of the law was questioned, and that by eminent legal authorities and professing churchmen. The thought was to get rid of what was felt to be a burden, by that means. That they did not attempt a straightforward repeal of the law, whatever the Proprietary might have said in the case, is proof that the church was very close to the hearts of the largest part of the people. That the Proprietary would have resisted such a repeal is probable, though by no means certain. He professed friendship for the church and the clergy, but what he cared for chiefly was that which promoted his own emoluments and pleasures.

The question of the poll tax was frequently discussed at this time. In 1747 the earlier law had been reenacted, making one-fourth of the amount payable in other produce than tobacco, at a fixed rate. This, like many of the colonial laws, was to continue in force only for a given time; the people, not having the right of repeal, thus retaining power over the laws in their own hands. Again, in 1753, the law was enacted to continue in force five years. And also again in 1758 and 1763. On this last occasion the law was further modified by making the poll to be thirty instead of forty pounds. Though this reduction imposed no real burden on the clergy; for owing to the great increase in population the salaries had generally so advanced as that the incomes in some instances were handsome, and in almost all parishes good. By this frequent presentation of the matter the question of salaries was kept alive in the people's minds, and so when any delinquency occurred among the clergy the matter was known far and wide. Such a case did occur a little later than our present period that shows the sensitiveness of the public feeling, and that the abuses of the system of the Establishment were working out their natural and fatal result. The Rev. Dr. Chandler, of New Jersey, distinguished subsequently to this by his activity as a champion of the church and church principles, was on a visit to Maryland, and he speaks about a condition of things that was very far from pleasing. The trouble was in Coventry Parish, which it was the desire of the people that the Doctor should receive, it being then vacant, and application was made to the Governor. Instead, however, of listening to them and presenting the man of their choice, who was also so eminently worthy, and thus pacifying a people who had formerly shown a restive spirit; possibly for that very reason he chose to ignore their desires; and that his lordship's prerogatives might be fully vindicated, forced upon the parish a man whom the people knew only too well as one wholly unfit for holy functions.

But the parishoners rose to the occasion and refused to receive the letter of induction offered, falling back upon what they esteemed their right of presentation. For they argued, that as the law was of their passing, and the church was sustained by their contributions, however provided, the parish was of necessity in their gift. Warm and acrimonious was the discussion that ensued, with even violence threatened, and that against the parson. The result was, however, that the people had to recede from their extreme position, and accept the order of things as it had been from the beginning. Mr. Henderson, formerly commissary, had held the view that the Bishop of London had the power to induct. Mr. Daniel Dulaney, who was the great legal authority in the colony at this time, as members of the same family were through several generations, showed that their claim had no ground in law, and that over and beyond the privileges that belonged to the Proprietary by his charter, the law of 1702 in plain terms put the right of presentation and induction in the governor's hands. Out of this difficulty there came other changes in the form of the letter of induction, as we shall see. It is said that this case was carried to England on appeal and decided in favor of the parish. What effect such a decision might have had does not appear, but things went on in this matter as they had been all along. This incident only shows that the troubles of the Establishment were now thickening, the people restive, the proprietary more exacting, and the colonial authorities just and honorable, but wanting in sympathy. The next ten years were to witness the further progress of these symptoms and eventuate in the death of the institution.

One of the instances that prove the unfortunate position of the church under the ungodly and presumptuous Proprietary, was his action in the year 1754. The clergy had not for years met together for conference, whether for mutual edification and protection, or for the promotion of the general welfare of the church. The governor did not summon them, as had been done earlier in the century, nor was there any commissary to gather them. Any meeting could only be accomplished by a common agreement, and they reached this in the year 1753. What was the occasion of their assembling then we do not know; possibly the further consideration at that time by the Assembly of the matter of reducing their salaries, though there were many things of common interest and general moment that they might find to discuss amongst themselves, and both they and the people would be the better for it. But how was their action regarded by his lordship? He professed a warm interest in both the church establishment and the clergy at this time. He immediately expressed to his governor his will and pleasure that they should not assemble again, and the governor of course issued notice of his lordship's desire. Truly we are living in different times from those when the church of God, as represented in her ministers, was subjected to such tyranny, the whim, the caprice of a young egotist who had only just reached his majority. And this was more than twenty years before the end came. That the clergy should have felt they were wearing a galling yoke could not help but be. The Establishment was to them sustained at a heavy cost of manhood; while the portents that indicated the future deliverance were as yet exceedingly indistinct, the cloud not even as large as a man's hand. The young administrator of such immense estate and weighty duties, may have had kind feelings for the church and clergy, but certainly he was exceedingly obtuse as to what would under the circumstances advance the church's best intrests.

The church, I have said, commanded no enthusiasm among the people or with the legislators now. Rather it was often jostled in debate and many unkind things said. On the the other hand, justice was meted out to it by the Assembly, and the comeliness of its circumstances was cared for by all its children. For we are now in the beginning of the period that was distinguished by the building of many of those structures that have so far withstood successfully the wear and tear of time, and will for centuries to come ; solid, substantial brick edifices generally, that are found in almost all parts of old Maryland. Romance or ignorance often makes them to have been built long before this, some of them, we are told, in 1692, the date when the Act of Establishment was first passed. But the records would show that most of those now standing were erected after the year 1748. And this would be probable for another reason, that previous to that time the parishes were too feeble, the population too sparse to have gone to the great expense necessary for such structures, as well as for the reason that structures of the size now found were not then necessary.

For it must be remembered how the means were provided. The people would first reach the conclusion that their church then standing was worn out, and no longer able to stand repairs ; or that the large increase in numbers demanded more ample room ; and most probably both causes would be found operating. Then a petition would be sent in to the legislature asking that a levy be imposed upon the parish, and this being done, the work was entrusted to the builders. The cost of such buildings would be from three to six thousand dollars, and sometimes probably more ; for some of the edifices are very large and handsome; plain enough as we count plainness, but striking memorials of the olden time. And this method of raising the means shows us the estimation in which the church was held through this troubled time. For first, that the people should have been content to assume so heavy a burden, proves their love and devotion to the church, and that the legislature would have been content to authorize such a heavy tax when often one-third of the residents within the parish were non-conformists, who could not help but be opposed to having their money taken from them for this purpose, proves that the institution as an establishment, was regarded with favor. And a blessed thing it was for Maryland after the depression of the revolution came on that these churches had been built; for for fifty years after that day the ideas and means were both most sadly cramped, and destitution would have been the result. As it was, God in his mercy so provided that the church survived, her children never wanted a place to assemble in for prayer and praise, and when a brighter day did dawn she was able again to enter upon a new career of prosperity.

The relative position of the church to the other religious bodies in the colony, both as to wealth and numbers, is approximately furnished us in an incident of the year 1760. There was but little intimate intercourse and no organic relation between the colonies at this time. There was, however, a strong fraternal feeling of sympathy, which doubtless the instinct of coming things strengthened; so that when in this year there was the great fire in Boston. Maryland was ready to extend any aid that might lie in her power. Fortunately the Governor issued a call for such aid, and the amount received astonishes us, remembering that Maryland had no city of pretentions save Baltimore and Annapolis, which were insignificant. The amount forwarded to the sufferers was over eighteen hundred pounds, being contributions in the churches, and of this members of the Establishment gave fifteen hundred pounds. These figures furnish evidence of why it was that the Legislature so readily granted the petitions for the heavy tax for the erection of new churches. The members of the Establishment were the wealthiest and most numerous in the province.

We have seen that in 1754 it pleased his lordship, the proprietor, to lay interdict upon the clergy, forbidding their coming together for conference, which was all that as citizens they were capable of doing. But this was not the worst evil he now inflicted, for about the same time he instructed Governor Sharpe that presentation to parishes should only be by his approval, thus taking from the governor an independence of action that sometimes would protect the church. The governor was so far stripped of responsibility, and doubtless degraded in his own eyes; for his lordship might over his cups give letters to boon companions, and for Maryland there was no deliverance. The old form of induction went on for a while, but the lord baron was the true power in the land. How far he exercised this control, we are not told, but for his favorites a place must as soon as possible be found.

In fact, Maryland was at this time an El Dorado for the parsons, and sometimes they were waiting, so many of them were there in the colony, until vacancies might occur. Some of them were employed as assistants, for division of parishes was greatly opposed by the incumbents, and by means of curates the desire of the people was sought to be appeased. Chapels of ease also were erected in outlying districts, out of which, from time to time, new parishes grew, for divisions did take place occasionally. There is no reason for supposing that the church was a heavy burden upon its members. Its misfortune was that it exacted from those who were unwilling to give. But for its members it was not a burden; for they only paid according to the males of their families and their profitable servants. The churchmen of Maryland to-day, of their own will and desire, contribute far more for religion than their fathers of those days did.

CHAPTER XV.

THE PARISH.

We have seen the urgency of the vestry to have their parish immediately provided for. Gov. Ogle, in response to their petition, granted the Rev. Charles Lake a letter of induction, February 23rd, 1748-49, who then began as the fourth rector of St. James' parish a ministry that reached to the year 1763, maintaining the general average of duration of rectorship that had held up to that time. Governor Ogle, as far as lay in his power, appointed good men to the parishes; though, unfortunately, the condition of things was often such that his best intentions were neutralized. Mr. Lake, however, as far as the record goes, seems to have fulfilled his best desires; for, unlike his two immediate predecessors, his ministry in the parish was without any occasion of dispute or dissatisfaction; a fact the more notable because his incumbency extended through a period when the tide of agitation ran high, when there were many squalls, if not violent tempests in the ecclesiastical atmosphere. These latter came on later, as in some instances they had also preceded this time. Doubtless, in many parishes throughout the province this was the case, the tide of peaceful life running on, the clergy confident of God's loving, fatherly care, and the people glad in every way to sustain their holy endeavors, unmindful of the jarring world without.

The form of the letter of induction which Mr. Lake presented was the same as that of his predecessor; after the recording of which he qualified as chief vestryman by taking the various oaths required. The rebellion of 1745 will here be remembered, the last effort of the Stuarts to recover the throne of England; and this will explain the stringency of the oaths of which we find a copy preserved in the church records. The first of these runs thus: I, A. B. do truly and sincerely acknowledge, profess, testify and declare, in my conscience before God and the world that our sovereign lord, King ———, is lawful and rightful King of the realm of England and all other his majesty's dominions and countries thereunto belonging; and I do solemnly and sincerely declare that I do believe in my conscience that the person pretended to be the Prince of Wales during the life of the late James, and since his decease pretending to be and taking upon himself the style and title of King of England, under the name of James III, hath not any right or title whatsoever to the crown of the realm of England, or of any other of the dominions thereunto belonging; and I do renounce, refuse and abjure any obedience to him. And I do swear that I will bear faith and true allegiance to his majesty King George, and him will defend to the utmost of my power, against all traitorous conspiracies and attempts whatsoever, which shall

be made against his person, crown, or dignity;
and I will do my best endeavor to disclose and
make known to his majesty and his successors,
all treason and traitorous conspiracies which I
shall know to be against him or any of them; and
I do faithfully promise, to the utmost of my
power, to support, maintain and defend the succession of the crown against him, the said James,
and all other persons whatsoever, as the same is
and stands limited by an act, entitled
an act declaring the rights and liberties
of the subject, and settling the succession of the
crown to his present majesty and the heirs of his
body being Protestants; and as the same by
another act, entitled an act for the further limitation of the crown and better securing the rights
and liberties of the subject, is and stands limited,
after the decease of her late majesty, and for default of issue of her late majesty, to the late
princess Sophia, electoress and Duchess Dowager of Hanover and the heirs of her body being
Protestants: and all these things I do plainly and
sincerely acknowledge and swear, according to
these express words by me spoken, and according
to the plain and common sense and understanding
of the same words, without any equivocation or
mental evasion or secret reservation whatsoever;
and I do make this recognition, acknowledgement, abjuration, renunciation and promise,
heartily, willingly and truly, upon the true faith
of a Christian.

So help me God.

The next oath we find recorded is as follows:
I do swear that I do from my heart abhor, detest
and abjure, as impious and heretical, that

damnable doctrine and position that princes excommunicated or deprived by the Pope, or any authority of the Church of Rome, may be deposed and murthered by their subjects or any other whatsoever. And I do believe that no foreign prince, person, prelate, state or potentate, hath or ought to have any jurisdiction, power, superiorty, pre-eminence, or authority, ecclesiastical or spiritual, within the kingdom of England or the dominion thereunto belonging.

So help me, &c.

A third oath was of a different tenor running thus: I, A. B. do swear that I will faithfully, honestly and justly nominate and recommend such person or persons to be an inspector or inspectors (of tobacco) as I think in my judgment and conscience is or are fit and capable to execute the office of an inspector or inspectors.

So help me, &c.

A fourth oath is as follows: I do solemnly swear and declare that I will justly and truly execute the office or trust of a vestryman of this parish, according to my best skill and knowledge, without prejudice, favor, or affection.

So help me, &c.

A fifth and last one is that which had been imposed from the beginning: We the subscribers do declare that we do believe that there is not any transubstantiation in the sacrament of the Lord's Supper or in the elements of Bread and Wine, at or after the consecration thereof by any person or persons whatsoever.

These oaths together bear in themselves a history and picture of the times, showing how the currents of feeling and conviction and fear were running. For the first and second were aimed at the lofty but well defined pretentions of the combined adversaries of English ecclesiastical and civil liberty, pretensions both of Pope and Prince that had more than once formulated themselves in the great argument of arms. The oaths were not framed against an imaginary danger, but one intensely real. These oaths also suggest why it was that the Roman Catholics were treated as they were during this period ; for, the adherents of a pope making extravagant claims, and the supposed friends of a house that for the religion they professed, were driven from England, and were now threatening the kingdom, they were looked upon as suspicious citizens who needed but the opportunity to excite them to the disturbance of the public peace. How far the fears were well grounded is another matter. Probably a little closer knowledge of the times would reveal that the house of Stuart and the pope had certain indiscreet adherents in the province who gave a stronger tone to the natural suspicion of the people. It is in fact stated that the repressive feature of the proposed supply bill during the French war had its origin in special ill feeling towards certain persons.

Also the oaths suggest to us rather different views of the duties and obligations of a vestryman from what are at present held; though the oath of allegiance, required at that time was continued down after the Revolution when the church ceased to be established, though it was then to the state of Maryland. The oaths do not bear the signatures of the vestrymen except that regarding transubstantiation, called "the test" to which alone signatures were required; a proper title, as it was used even to test a man's qualification for the ballot, the Roman Catholics being by that means excluded. They were all, however, taken by vestrymen as "prescribed by law," and they continued to be taken down to the American Revolution. And we can see readily how during the period immediately preceding that event, when men's minds were anticipating the necessity of revolt, such an oath as the first given, if taken by all the vestrymen through many years, should have acted as a restraint against that precipitancy that characterized some of the provinces. For Maryland was loth to take the final step and preserved her loyalty to the last moment; she would not sunder the ties that bound her to the mother country until nothing else was possible. The church was thus to Maryland a conservative influence. Also we can understand how in addition to the force of education, the clergy, having bound themselves by such solemn oaths, should have found it difficult, and in so many cases impossible, to cast in their fortunes with the newly created state, and have preferred to return to the mother country.

The most important thing that happened in the parish during this period was the building of the new church. For this was the era of church building in Maryland, most of the old structures that had been erected about the beginning of the century, having by this time worn out; having also, many of them, been so modified to meet the growing population, that they were hardly capable of any further enlargement. Almost all the more worthy structures of Maryland, whatever tradition may say, were at this time erected. Most of the first buildings had been of frame, the erection of them even having been a burden to the scant population. Though not only wooden buildings had decayed within that period, for if we are to take old St. Anne's of Annapolis, as speaking by its next friend, Rev. Mr. Boucher, as witness, even brick walls had not been proof against the attacks of time.

"How changed the times, for now all round
Where numbered stately piles abound,
All better built, and looking down
On one quite antiquated grown:
Left unrepaired, to time a prey,
I feel my vitals fast decay:
And often I have heard it said
That some good people are afraid
Lest I should tumble on their head;
Of which, indeed, this seems a proof,
They seldom come beneath my roof."

The matter of a new church was first agitated in the year 1760, when a thorough examination having been made, the old church, having fulfilled its holy purposes for sixty years, was declared incapable of standing much longer. Besides, the taxables of the parish having increased from about five hundred to about twelve hundred, there could hardly have been room for all that came to worship. The next step was to petition the Assembly for a levy upon all the inhabitants of the parish; and the response being favorable, on the twenty-second of June in 1762 an advertisement was inserted in the Annapolis paper for bidders. As it turned out the plan was drawn by one of the vestrymen, James Trotter, who received for the same fifteen pounds currency, eleven pounds five shillings sterling, and the building was contracted for by another one, Mr. John Weems. The notice of the contract reads thus: "Likewise Mr. John Weems, has undertaking the building of a breek church in the sd Parrish according to the draft of the plan that was this day layd before the vestry, and is to build the sd church att fourteen hundred pounds cur. (one thousand and fifty pounds sterling,) without any further charges to the said parrish in any shape whatever, in case that the vestry git ann act of Assembley for what tob. will be wanting of the sum that is to build the said church; for as thay hant tob. enufe in hand for the finniching of the sd church." Evidently the schoolmaster was not abroad. Rather his presence was sorely needed in the parish. The church was three years in building.

The amount granted by the Assembly was one hundred and thirty thousand pounds of tobacco, to be collected in two levies, and the work began. Fortunately the builder was honest, and the building that he thus associated with his name, a name notable in other ways beside, will for many a day be a monument to his memory. The architecture is plain, of course, the interior without galleries. Some parish churches of the period had these, possibly for the servants, though now they are disused, and are a blemish. Whether the bricks came from England we do not know, for the work was done by contract, and no bill of items was rendered. Though there was no need of going to England for them, as there was clay in abundance near at hand, out of which bricks had been made a half century before. The interior arrangements were according to the order of the time, and the old fashioned, high back, square family pews are still remembered by some of the old people. The pulpit stood in the middle of the long side on the North, with the chancel in the East end. This was the more common way, though some of the churches, as All Saints', Calvert County, had the pulpit at the West end and the chancel at the East. The ceiling of the church is arched, the windows large, and everything is in due proportion. The dimensions are forty by sixty feet, and the walls are massive. A substantial porch of brick with three arched openings and about eight feet square, covers the South door. Standing quietly in the midst of the churchyard, surrounded with many splendid trees under which are resting, in the hope of the resurrection, the mortal remains of those whose voices once rose in prayer and praise from its hallowed walls to heaven, it is a worthy object of our love and admiration.

Another matter that occupied the attention of the vestry, and whose importance is presented to us by the building of the church, was the question of parish lines; for it was a question of considerable moment to a man on which side of a line he lived when nearly fifteen hundred pounds were to be raised by the sheriff; for the church cost in all fourteen hundred and forty-two pounds. By 1751 the old lines of 1695 had become effaced. Barns and quarters had rotted away within that time, and the St. James' people thought that the South River parish people were not acting fairly, but were "abusing" them.

And so they called in the great light "Mr. Dulany Jr." to plead their cause and have the lines determined. Whether it was done we do not know, or whether the South River people went on "abusing" them, as is highly probable. But it has not only for a special levy that the determination of the question was advisable. The parson suffered when the other parish got what did not belong to it; and so we find the parson of St. James' joining in the endeavor to restrain the encroaching tendencies of the South River neighbor.

The parish records throughout this period show a thoughtful care on the part of the vestry for the church and its surroundings. The church was old enough now to be endeared to them by fond memories, as the place where parents and grandparents, friends, brothers and sisters gone on before, had made the rich offerings to God of their hearts and minds. It was the centre also of life's better activities, far more may be than the church is anywhere now; for there were not as many subjects to engross the mind and affections then as now; though, of course, the devil's allurements were just as seductive to those who were not devoted to the faith. The vestry felt the power of the oath which they had taken, and were diligent in their duties ; sometimes it would appear, even to a narrow rigidness that wore a hard and forbidding aspect, as when within two months of Mr. Lang's death, in the fall of the year when the glebe was profitless save as a residence, they sent the church warden to the widow to demand of her compensation for the same "to lessen the charges accruing to the parish." They did it, they said "to comply with their oath"; but conscience sometimes can constrain a pitiless narrowness that is contemptible. Also on another occasion we find them solemnly dividing and standing three to three, whether they should allow a contractor for two pairs of hinges for the church gate. The parson stood on the side of liberality, but the man lost his money. In 1751 the church came into possession of the handsome silver baptismal bowl that had been devised by William Loch some twenty years before. The cause of the the delay does not appear, as the administrator of the estate seems to have paid on demand. A "pedestal" was ordered to be made on which the bowl might be set. We also find at this time the old item reappearing of "stocks and whipping post," the church premises being graced with them as a permanent institution. Unlike New England customs, however, they were still reserved only for those who could not assert their respectability as a bar, and doubtless the misdemeanor that caused the infliction was something more heinous than kissing one's wife on the street on Sunday. For this offence in Massachusetts could be atoned for by nothing less than a plentiful laying on of the lash.

Among other items now mentioned is an order " for two yards of cloth for a communion cloth, and fringe suitable for the same," evidently an altar cloth such as we have seen in the beginning of the century, and such as we also later down find still provided. We have also in 1754 the following articles delivered by the rector to the vestry, " one silver flagon, one silver challace, one silver dish, one silver bason, one silver salver, two supplaces, one silk hood, one table cloth, one napkin." The hood indicates that a man of learning had been in charge of the parish, most probably the Rev. Mr. Lang. The orthography of the word surplice was as uncertain then to registrars as it has often since been to some other persons, we having within a few pages, beside the above, "surplus," "surplias" and "surpelias."

We also have through eight years, the vestry returning to the county court lists of the bachelors in the parish to be taxed under the supply bill of 1755 which has been already noticed. However far it may have been one of the objects of the law to exercise a constaining force upon this fraternity to make them change their estate, certainly it in a large measure failed of attaining its purpose, as the record shows. The age of persons liable was not to be less than twenty-five years, up to which point they seemed not to have been regarded as responsible, and notable is the eagerness with which those returned would claim their minority if possible. Also if a man could fix his income below the taxable rate, he was ever forward to plead his poverty. To abate a nuisance, however, the law does not seem to have had much power; for while indeed the number returned in 1757 was twenty which fell off in 1759 to twelve, yet in 1763 we find it gone up again to eighteen, ten of whom were returned as having an income of three hundred pounds and over. Something was amiss. The days were not marrying days, for the number thus given was large to the whole number of the people. The income was ample. Possibly eligible parties of the other part were wanting. Of the eighteen, five had continued steadfast throughout, defying the powers both of attraction and constraint. It is noticeable as justifying the supposition that the other parties necessary to the marriage contract were not to be had, that no attempt was made to tax them; though it may have been regarded as a hopeless matter to attempt to verify the age; and also, as it was perceived that the law was an imposition for delinquency, it may have been felt to be unjust to lay it on the maidens.

The Rev. Mr. Lake, whose ministry in the parish ceased in 1763, probably kept a school, as so many of the rectors did throughout the province, thus by this means also assisting the welfare of the people; for with a scanty public school system, with but one school in each county, the opportunities of the people were small, while the standard of scholarship in such schools was low. A parish school, therefore, taught by the rector, who was often a scholarly man, was a great blessing, and helped greatly in creating and preserving a higher and better tone in society. Mr. Lake, also, evidently kept his school in the vestry house, which stood in the church yard. This was felt by the vestry to be improper, and so in April, 1764, we find the following entry: "This vestry agrees that no choole shall be kept in the vestry house of St. James' parrish." Most evidently it needed to be kept somewhere if the registrar's training was a sign of the times. The same registrar recording the notice of his own election in 1763, writes as follows: "Benj. Lane is to continue clarke of the Ridg't for the insuing yeare at seven hundred and fifty pounds of tob. and if the vestry hant tobac. enufe then the said Lane is to be paid at 12s. 6d. in purposion to what the sd vestry shall receive."

After the departure of Mr. Lake from the parish there was no rector for about one year, during which time nothing was done except the building of the new church, which, of course, occupied a great deal of attention. Possibly the church was occasionally supplied as formerly it had been; or possibly the governor waited for a voice from over the water. Governor Sharpe had come into the province bringing his commission in 1753. In the removal of Governor Ogle the church lost a friend. Governor Sharpe, while in many respects an admirable character, was evidently also a man of worldly policy, and the administration of the church at his hands was frequently without any due sense of the vast obligations belonging to his office. Parishes were given away without any respect for the preferences or protests of the people, and without any regard for the unfitness of the candidate for his bounty. He remained about fifteen years in office.

CHAPTER XVI.

THE FIFTH PERIOD.

The period upon which we now enter was the most active in all the colonial history, not of Maryland only but of all America. For it was the period during which the great questions were agitated that finally resulted in the declaration of American independence. These began soon after, and were in no slight degree dependent upon, the extinction of the French Empire in Canada, the same removing what had always been a cause of more or less anxiety to the colonists, making them look to England for assistance. In another way also did this loss to the French promote the American revolution; for it was in part the heavy burdens which the French war created, that caused the British government to look to the provinces for pecuniary assistance.

But over and above all other causes, the agitation of that last decade that resulted in American freedom, arose from within. The colonies, that had grown up as children, though without much maternal care from the home government, which always thought more of British profits than of the welfare of the provinces, had now reached the age of manhood, and sensitive in regard to everything that did not comport with their strength and vigor, they looked with suspicion upon every proposed measure of the British Ministry, however much precedent might seem to justify it. The course of Dr. Franklin in London evidences this, for he seconded measures there that were violently repudiated at home.

The manhood of the American colonies, however, did not show itself only in the way of jealousy of British measures. It was the maturity of a peculiar civilization in which various things had been outgrown which up to that time had been looked upon as essential component parts of a duly organized society. The training of the colonies had been peculiar, different from anything in the past history of states. They had been the voluntary creation of individuals on remote shores, with a home government too much occupied in its own affairs to give any heed to them. They had made their own laws, provided for their own defence, determined in many things their own government. They were even in large measure separated one from the other, not only by non-intercourse, but also by very marked characteristics. So that a strong spirit of self-confidence and self-assertion was engendered among them in respect of one another. They ministered to British prosperity through the commerce they furnished, while they often felt they received no adequate return for the impositions they had to bear.

Under these circumstances an independent spirit was developed in them, and a suspicious disposition towards everything that seemed to affect their independence; so that for a score of years and more before the final rupture, their history was one of watchful protest against some dreaded usurpation, whether the province was a royal one, or whether it was proprietary. Theirs was a civilization in which individuality and the private rights and liberty of the citizen, were the most eminent conception, the contrary of the leading thought of royalty. And this was in a marked degree the condition of things in Maryland, where human rights and the true relations of the citizen to the government, as between the people and Lord Baltimore, had always engaged a large degree of attention. Taxation and the right of the people to make their own laws, jealousy against prerogative, government by the people for the people, these subjects agitated the people of Maryland along with all the rest of America, through this period, kindling it into a flame, as testified to by a resident of this province then.

And the result was what, may be, no one foresaw, from this great leading consideration, a great broadening out of sympathies and a laying hold of principles which in themselves are the first basis of all right government. So that when under the common agitation the issue at last was reached, Puritan New England, Quaker Pennsylvania, Church of England Maryland and Virginia, were found in substantial agreement, and all the differences that had existed, whether under statute or not, as to the ground of citizenship, ceased to be. All churches were dis-established and church rates abolished; and even the

Roman Catholic, no longer feared under the clearer light that had at length dawned, was everywhere accorded equal rights with all other men. And doubtless one cause why the Church of England was disturbed so greatly during the last decade of her existence as an establishment, why some of her most prominent sons in the controversies of the time, lifted up the heel against her as an establishment, was that the times were out of harmony with such an institution. It was a burden because it was, though as yet not perceived by the citizens of Maryland, abnormal, a violation of the true relations that exist between men in society. That any man should be disfranchised because of his religion or his want of it, or that one man should be taxed to provide min istrations and a house of worship for another, for which he himself had an aversion, whether conscientious or not, was contrary to the developing sense of American freedom.

That the church through this time had a great trial of afflictions none need question, and that without any offence or fault of her own. That she was still afflicted with some evil men was true, and that her clergy were frequently out of sympathy with the people in the great questions which the people had received as a birthright, but of which the clergy, as coming into the province only in the full years of manhood, were ignorant. Also many of the clergy, nearly one-half, were foreigners to the colonists, who chiefly sprang from English stock; for Scotchmen and Irishmen were then, even much less than now, in harmony with the English ideas and English feelings inherited by the colonists. Also, as not having been chosen by, but imposed upon the people, there was no mutual sense of dependence. Rather the clergy represented an extraneous power of whose every act they were jealous, which was also at this time disposed ever to assume a more imperious tone and to be more reckless of propriety in church administration, and who only resisted the introduction of Episcopacy lest it should interfere with its own untramelled influence. Unfortunately also circumstances brought the church into conflict with public sentiment at a time when the mind of the public was violently excited by other questions.

The great agitation of the year 1765 will here be remembered, and the energetic action of Maryland in common with the rest of the colonies. The spontaneous outburst of that time was only a witness to hidden fire. And the fire never went out afterwards; for there was enough in British measures, whether they were proposed or repealed, to excite the people's alarm. Here will also be remembered the great excitement produced by the Proclamation act of 1770, when the Governor attempted to regulate by his own manifesto the fees to be paid the officers of the provincial government; an assumption to resist which the people had been prepared for many years. For Maryland had to contend against a twofold encroachment, both of the English government and also of her superior Lord and his governors. All kinds of tyranny excited her, but especially that of petty tyrants.

Unfortunately, therefore, for the church, in the year 1767, the question of the induction of the clergy assumed large proportions, particularly because his excellency the Governor in the plentitude of his power, saw fit not only to ignore the people's pleasure in not appointing the man they preferred, but in appointing the one they reprobated One parish even proceeded to extremity and refused to receive the letter of induction, and the matter, taken out of parochial bounds became a general question. The courts of the province decided in favor of the Governor's unlimited right, and his position was sustained by the best legal talents of the day. The people however, did not know how to yield, and somewhat inconsistently with their patriotic claims, carried the matter to England. But Lord Baltimore went on inducting whom he would. This question was strongly agitated in various parishes, and private terms were attempted by the vestries. Doubtless had not the Revolution cut all matters short the evils of the system would have necessarily been remedied in a very few years. For it would not have been possible for any one, and certainly not for one whose character could not command the public esteem, as Frederick, the last of his name, to wantonly commit such outrage upon the people's highest interests. The remedy would have been found before long under any circumstances.

The old question that had been coming to the surface all through the century, and particularly when the waters were troubled, again at this time was presented, the question of a bishop for the colonies. And nothing exhibits more strongly the great yearning desire of the clergy for a better condition of things in the church. For they all felt that not only was the effect of the delinquent, whoever he might be, had upon his own work, but that all the clergy of the province were hindered and their work marred by the evil reports that got abroad. And, therefore, their urgency for this relief. But, unfortunately, they were the only persons in the colonies that had strong faith in that means, and who did not look upon the remedy as fraught with greater ills than it was intended to correct. Therefore, also, at this time they were again strongly opposed. First it was by his lordship's agent, Governor Sharpe, who in 1767 rejected the notion on the ground that it would interfere with his lordship's rights, while Governor Eden afterwards assumed a more supercilious tone, insisting that a bishop, if appointed and resident in the colony, would be able to effect nothing, because the parishes of Maryland were "donatives," over the holders of which the Bishop could have no control. Lord Baltimore in one word, would appoint whom he would, and neither his wickedness nor his mistakes should be corrected, however much the people's spiritual welfare might suffer. Dr. Hawks, however, who argues this question, shows that even being donatives, the claims of Governor Eden were false, because a clergyman holding such a living, was liable to discipline for evil manners. Gov. Eden, further chose to assume a supercilious bearing towards the clergy.

But unfortunately the people at this time cordially endorsed the action and the opinions of the Governors. For as Eddis tells us in his fourth letter written in 1770, "the colonists were strongly prejudiced against the Episcopal order."

their imaginations clothing a Bishop in the colonies with the extreme functions and prerogatives that their Lordships possessed in England, a form of power that they both dreaded and hated. We have seen also in a previous period, that people in England equally opposed the Episcopate for America on the ground that it would affect unfavorably the dependence of the colonies upon the mother country. So to the last hour of the existence of the establishment there was a harmony of antagonism everywhere to this proposition, which was found amongst all parties on no other subject; doubtless so ordered in God's good providence.

And yet there was a cry for discipline. There was a strong desire for some corrective means, and again there was advanced the old scheme that had before repeatedly failed. This was the appointment of a mixed court under an act of the Assembly, for the trial of the clergy. This was first attempted in 1708, but the Governor immediately disallowed it, the clergy bringing a strong pressure to bear. Again in 1724 the attempt had been made, but with like result, the clergy objecting to the trial of any of their order by laymen; claiming that such was against the principles of the church of which they were ministers. Again in 1768 the attempt was made, the Governor, as ordinary, having by the bill disciplinary power granted him with power to associate with himself three clergymen and three laymen. But again the clergy objected, showing, in addition to the former argument about the principles of the church, that such power would interfere with the civil rights of his Lordship in the matter of the livings; and the consequence again was that the Governor did not approve. The clergy offered, in a memorial to the Assembly, to frame a law which should be effective, and at the same time obviate these objections, but their proposition was ignored. As we shall see, the clergy, who could be so strenuous for the rights of their order now, could also ignore the principles on which they laid such stress. The clergy were a third estate in the province, and were regarded with jealousy by both the other parties.

An instance of this jealousy on the part of the Proprietary was given in 1769. The movement for obtaining the Episcopate about that time had been a general one on the part of the clergy in the several provinces, and the Maryland clergy had acted only upon the invitation of their brethren. Having consulted together they had come to a like conclusion with them. This combined action was feared as a precedent apparently, by his Lordship, and at this time an order was issued by the Governor forbidding the clergy to assemble on any occasion. This was a favorite means of the Proprietary, he having done the same in 1754. The clergy evidently did not regard his mandate as of any great force, for they did meet as we have seen in 1769. By what right he should have attempted to interdict their assembling is difficult for us to perceive. To our ideas such an attempt can only appear as an extravagant outrage. It was a stretch of prerogative that could only excite the bitterest feeling both for its illegality and its injustice.

But misfortunes had not yet begun to cease.

Suspicion and contumely had been heaped upon the clergy, most of whom were an honor both to their calling and to manhood. Yet there was still reserved a bitterness of trial equal to if not greater than any yet passed through. This was in connection with what is known as the Proclamation and Vestry act question, which began in 1770, the origin of which was as follows: It had been the custom in Maryland as well as in the other colonies, for the Assembly, in passing money bills, to limit the time of their operation, with the intention of keeping by this means the officers of the government dependent upon their will. In Maryland also, the state of the currency made such a thing of two-fold value, the price of tobacco being exceedingly variable. With this limitation the inspection bill of 1763 had been passed, the same providing for the fees of certain offices, which were paid in tobacco, as all fees were, unless the one paying should prefer to pay in money at a fixed rate of commutation. This law was passed to hold only till 1770, when the attempt was made by the lower house to renew it, with certain modifications in the matter of fees. For the enormous sum frequently exacted was an unwarrantable imposition upon the people, and the aggregate in various instances altogether out of proportion to the duty and responsibility of the officer.

The law, however, did not pass; for the upper house, some of whose members were the recipients of much fees, objected, and the Assembly came to a dead-lock. It was soon found also, that an accommodation was impossible, and the Assembly was prorogued. In this emergency Governor Eden saw fit to issue a proclamation providing for the fees of office, appointing those that had been named in the law of 1763 to which the people had so violently objected. Then began the war of words and the reign of bitterness, not only the amount of fees being exclaimed against, but also, the principle assumed by the Governor that he could of himself regulate such an important matter as the fees of office; that is, by his own act assess taxes upon the people. His excuse was, and the defence made by his supporters, that he was justified in his act by the absence of any provision for the emergency. But this did not in any way satisfy the people, and the battle lasted till the year 1773.

Now most unfortunately the church was immediately associated with this great agitation, though it was some relief that the Governor did not intervene in its behalf. For the same law of 1763 that regulated officers fees provided also for a reduction of the poll tax levied for the benefit of the church, the reduction being one fourth of the amount fixed by the original law of 1702. When, however, the law of 1763 lapsed, while the officers fees became an open question, the clergy insisted that the provision made for the establishment by the law of 1702 again came in force, as that law does not seem in any of its clauses to have been repealed; only this supplementary act seems to have been passed. And in this their opinion they were ably sustained by some of the best legal talent of the day. Again, however, it was their bad lot to have the same advocates on their side as had defended the proclamation act; so that their influence was very much weakened, while some of the sons of the church were among her most vigorous and able antagonists. But it was not only a battle of the lawyers. The clergy themselves did right manful service, notably the Rev. Mr. Boucher, whose stalwart spirit could give as heavy blows as he was called on to receive, and his thrusts were sometimes well aimed, not only at the cause of his opponents, but passed through the joints of their armor, as when he reminded some of them that the very law that they were endeavoring to overwhelm, was one which as vestrymen they were daily recognizing and honoring.

For there loomed up in the midst of the contest the question whether the vestry act of 1702 was or ever had been a law at all; the plea being that King William, in whose name the writs calling the assembly ran, had died before the coming together of the same, and therefore that that assembly was illegal and all its acts void. Of course such a question excited everyone, and with the numerous opponents of the law in the colony, that is, the dissenters of all names, with some churchmen joined with them, and with the whole body of the ungodly and the profane, it was a heavy blow at the Establishment. Whether the facts were as stated, and whether the law was null supposing the facts true, was never determined; for in 1773 in the month of November, an accommodation was reached, thirty pounds of tobacco being fixed as the poll tax, with the privilege granted the people of commuting at four shillings per poll. The proviso, however, was added that such a provision should in no way prejudice the question about the validity of the law of 1702. Whether that was a sop thrown to the dissenters, because the church was so strong and zeal for its support so great as that fear was felt about destroying the Establishment, or whether it was proposed to keep it an open question for final determination, we do not know. Most probably, however, it was only the sop, and the church was loved and cherished by the vast mass of the people. For it was a crime to exact the tax a moment longer of Roman Catholics, Quakers, and all that race, if the law was not binding, and the bitterness of the controversy for three years, in which the question might have been settled, had prepared the people for any extreme step that might be esteemed justifiable. Besides, when three years after this the Establishment did cease, the state separated from her companion with a tender and generous salutation. The proviso, therefore, in all probability, was only a peace offering to a very influential minority.

But even these questions were only incidental to a great raging sea of excitement whose waters were swelling all this time; an excitement produced by the question of stamped paper, the question of non-importation of British goods, the question of sympathy with the other colonies, the question of the destruction of the tea in the Annapolis harbor; questions over which not only were the people excited, but which caused them to organize for the promotion of the ends they were determined on and about which they were very clear minded. And again to our sorrow we find a large part of the clergy divided off from the people. "All America," said Eddis, "is in a flame. I hear strange language every day. The colonists are rife for any measrues that will tend to the preservation of what they call their natural liberty." To be antagonistic to the people at that time and on that subject, meant ostracism, and it meant violence too, if the opposition of the clergy should show itself in crossing the people's will in any way, even in the matters concerning religion, or the worship of the house of God. And this could not be avoided; for as it has always been found, granting any measure of religiousness in a man's temperament, let a great crisis arrive and that man will flee to the Almighty if it is only to propitiate Him to become auxiliary for the furtherance of his desires.

And so at this time, we are told, that out of the forty-five parishes in Maryland, twenty-eight became vacant at the Revolution, and that only twenty-five of the clergy are reported to have taken the oath of fidelity to the state. How many of these were only half-hearted in the cause and so did not command the confidence or respect of their people, we are not told, but probably a considerable ratio according to a general rule that has often been tested; for it was a sore temptation to a clergyman then, dependent on his parish for his daily bread, far away from the home country where only, and then only probably, maintenance could be found for him and his little ones, it was a sore temptation to him to take the oath, though with many qualms of conscience; and that so many refused to do it, but surrendered their livings, enduring every

necessary discomfort and loss for conscience
sake, is a high testimony to their christian man-
liness. It was a trial similar to that of St. Bar-
tholomew's day 1662 or to that of 1643 when the
covenant was imposed; and what they endured
in every way that refused the test, was equal to
the burden of those earlier times. For it was not
only the loss of church and livelihood, but they
were placed under the social ban, and their lives
made uncomfortable. For in those days in any
part of America to sympathize with the king as
against the colonies, made one to be regarded as
a traitor and a public enemy.

We get some glimpse of the condition of things
in the experience of the Rev. Mr. Boucher,
before spoken of; though, doubtless, his heroic
fortitude was not emulated by many, and so but
few, if any, had to bear his extreme discomfort.
His parish was in Prince George's county, given
him at the time, he made himself famous by his
controversy with Messrs. Paca and Chase over
the vestry act question. Here he remained till
the bitterness of the times brought things to a
climax. This was reached in 1775, when he tells
us: "For more than six months I preached,
when I did preach, with a pair of loaded pistols
lying on the cushion, having given notice that if
any man or any body of men could possibly be
so lost to all sense of decency or propriety as to
drag me out of my own pulpit I should think
myself justified before God and man in repelling
violence." Probably the young man's violent
self-assertion begot the violence that was shown
towards him; nevertheless he was sincere and
felt with terrible earnestness on the subject that
was agitating every one.

But in May of this year his belligerancy became even more pronounced. The eleventh day of that month had been appointed a day of fasting and of prayer, and Mr. Boucher let it be known that he would preach in his church. His text, Neb. vi. 10, 11, shows the nature of the man, and it is extremely improbable that his highest eloquence would have accomplished any good with that theme. He did not, however, then have an opportunity of delivering his mind of its burden. For coming to the church about fifteen minutes before the time for beginning the service, he found that already his curate, who was a Republican, was in the desk, and that a crowd of men were around the church doors. On attempting to enter the leader of the people approached him, saying they did not want him to preach, when he replied that he would either do it or lose his life. The people, however, did not look upon that as the alternative. In the mean time he had gotten into the church and attempted, with his pistol in one hand and his sermon in the other to reach the pulpit. Finding that impossible, however, and being surrounded by the excited crowd, he seized the leader by the collar, and told him, with his pistol cocked, that if anyone should dare attack him he would blow his, the leader's, brains out. But the men were as stubborn as he was, and while respecting him enough not to hurt him, they escorted him out of church and all the way home, and with music, too, though it was by the fifer playing the rogue's march. There was evidently a good deal of humor in that crowd. Mr. Boucher, however, was not intimidated, for on the next

Sunday he went to the church, and though amidst great confusion, preached his fast-day sermon. Mr. Boucher afterwards went to England when the difficulties of the situation multiplied, and there spent the remainder of his life in a comfortable parish, and used his talented pen not only on American affairs, but besides the special work of his holy calling, also on matters of philological science.

It was in the midst of such agitation as this, though not generally so violent, as there was but one Mr. Boucher in the province, that the establishment at last came to an end. The developing spirit of liberty, that either directly or indirectly caused all this agitation, fully expressed itself when at last the proprietary government was overthrown, all allegiance to a foreign authority was repudiated, and the people made their own laws and established their own principles of government. For the first element of that spirit of liberty was equality under the law, and the common enjoyment of all franchises; every man being accorded the full possession of the same until by his own unworthiness he had been adjudged unfit.

With this apprehension on the part of people the establishment of necessity ceased to be; for the principle that lay at the bottom of it, was that all should contribute to the support of an institution that before the law had no exclusive value; for freedom to worship was always granted in Maryland to every name and sect, the Roman Catholics being only politically disfranchised. And this support they were compelled to render, though to do so they felt to be a violation of their own rights of property, as well as in some instances, a violation of conscience. The establishment was an institution that had outlived its day in America ; and so as soon as the authorities passed upon the principles of the new government, which they did in the convention that closed its sessions November 11, 1776, the establishment passed out of existence. This was by the Declaration of Rights which set forth the plainest and simplest principles of civil and religious liberty. The state, however, was tender towards its old associate ; for instead of subjecting it to the outrage which befell the church in Virginia, the glebes, churches, chapels and other property then owned, were secured to her, and also it was provided that the repairs of sacred edifices then in progress under former acts should still go on. The incumbents also of the parishes were to be paid up to November 1st. And further, the declaration recognized that it was legitimate to provide by a tax for the support of the christian religion, with the right of every individual, however, to say to the support of what denomination his money should be applied. This is interesting as showing that the church establishment with all its drawbacks, had not excited that animosity for a state support of religion that the outcry of the time might have led us to anticipate. Rather there is no reason for believing but that the church was very profoundly the church of the affections of the people, and that she only ceased to be the establishment because such an external relation was not in keeping with the sentiments of the times. The church of England was always the church of the peoples' desire, and the best and ablest citizens, with a rare exception, were her children. And because of the love borne her then, and the traditions she has inherited from that time, the church in Maryland holds the eminent position now of having, save in one case, a larger percentage to the whole population than the church in any other state, a fact the more notable when we remember to how relatively small a degree the people are gathered together in towns where the church mostly flourishes. The rural districts of Maryland are covered by old parishes where there abounds a traditional as well as personal love of the church, a love that has often survived through periods of the most adverse circumstances.

CHAPTER XVII.

THE PARISH.

St. James' parish presents to us during this period in various things a minor picture of what was going on in the colony at large, being disturbed by some of the causes that so deeply affected other churches. It presents, also, some attractive features, and so doubtless is a fair representation of the whole. The Rev. Alex. Adams succeeded to the rectorship September the fourth, 1764, presenting his letter bearing that date. He was probably a very good man, for he had been a long while in the province, and is described as very old. A bad man whose reputation would have been too well known through a forty years residence, would not have been able to secure such a parish as St. James' at that time of life. It is a comfort to remember that he who in 1723 was compelled to record such a hard fate as his fortune, debt, destitution and anxiety, should have been able to spend his last days in peace; for in 1767 when he died, St. James parish was reported to be worth three hundred pounds per annum. This was from all sources, probably, as another estimate places the amount at two hundred and thirteen pounds, three shillings, which was received from the tax. Other parishes received at this time. St. John's, Baltimore county, three hundred and sixty-four pounds; St. Paul's, Baltimore county, two hundred and eleven pounds; St. Anne's, A. A. Co., one hundred and ninety-nine pounds; Port Tobacco, St. Mary's county, two hundred and fifty-three pounds; All Saints, Calvert county, one hundred and seventy-three pounds. Some parishes received even more. Mr. Adams was the third rector who died during his incumbency.

It was while he was in the parish that the Church was finally completed, being delivered up by the contractor in 1765, Dec. 17th. The first intention had been to provide only twenty-six pews, but this was found to be inadequate and so the number was increased to forty. It may be consoling to some persons to know that the pews were sold, becoming the private and exclusive property of certain persons; certainly a curious feature under an establishment. Aug. 6th, 1765, we have the following entry: "Likewise agreed by this vestry that Mr. Sam. Chew is to have the south-east pew in the church ajoyning to the aulter, and the sd. Chew is to pay the vestry fifteen pounds current money for the same." This Chew is the same man that about two years after this accepted a challenge from the minister of the parish and went to the duelling ground to meet him. He was a vestryman. His proximity to the "aulter" does not seem to have taught him self sacrifice.

The new building would seem to have given a deal of satisfaction to the vestry, who entered upon possession with the determination to preserve everything in order and peace. Also, they were firmly resolved to protect private rights in the pews; for Dec. 31st, 1765, two weeks after having received the building, they passed this resolution: "This vestry agreed that if any person should intrude or come into any person or persons' pews without being asked, such person applying to the church warden or vestrymen (they) are to take such person that may intrude, (who) shall be put in the stockes, which the vestry agrees that a pare of stocks shall be erected att the church for that purpus." The grammar and the spelling are worthy of the cause. Who they were that might be so treated we are not told, but evidently "respectability" could not save them if complaint were entered by the pew-holder. It was an eminently peculiar way of receiving a seeker after the way of life; and doubtless it was highly edifying to the favored pew-holders to see such interlopers dragged out of the house of God, and the act of doing so promoted decorum and propriety within the hallowed walls. And then their righteous souls were satisfied, as passing by the culprit on their return from worship, they saw how such presumption and wickedness found its due reward at the hands of the officers of the sacred house. The modern method of accomplishing the same end of ejecting and punishing such "intruders" is different and much more graceful, but just as effective for preventing the misdemeanor. It is to walk up to your pew door with as much ostentation as you can command, stand there, look surprised at the "intruder," budge not an inch, but frown on him until he has taken up his hat, arrested himself, and carried himself out of the "church," filled with anger at you and contempt for your religion. That is the modern way, and it is just as effective and a great deal more refined than the horrid stocks. But we do not believe those old men ever acted under that resolution. The parson was not present when it was passed, and only a bare working number of the vestry. It was doubtless a dead letter from the beginning. For poor and rich, "black" brethren and white, have always been welcomed within St. James' sacred walls.

The vestry felt no hesitation about calling for money at this time, notwithstanding the fact that there had been recently such a very great outlay; but from year to year a levy was asked for and obtained for the maintenance and repair of the church building and its surroundings. This levy varied according to the needs of the year, being at one time five pounds of tobacco per poll at another two, at another three. The tobacco also, that accrued during an interregnum, went under the law, into the hands of the vestry, to be used for parish purposes, nor as far as we can see, were the vestries called on at this time to give an account of how such funds had been laid out. Possibly the clergy absorbed all the public attention that was bestowed upon the church. There is scarcely, however, room for doubt that they used their resources discreetly, for had they not, there was plenty of watchful eyes that would have discerned the delinquency. The church came in for little or no opprobrium in those insolent days. The clergy got it all, surely a high testimony of the church's firm position in the general estimation. Were the clergy only the scapegoat for the people's ill will that could not so readily otherwise be expressed? Did a turbulent minority attempt thus to wreak vengeance as the only open means to express their animosity? The sad feature is that any of the clergy were found so derelict as to give a handle for such ill feeling to take hold of.

The vestry spent liberally on the church building and all that belonged to it, keeping everything in good order and taking pride in doing so. In the year 1768 they proposed quite an extensive outlay in painting the church, enclosing the churchyard, and building a new vestryhouse. The money for this purpose, however, was to come from a new source, a private agreement with the Rev. Walter Magowan, who was then serving as a minister in the parish. It will be remembered that at this time the question of ministerial support was agitating the colony; one of the features of which was that the vestries tried to make private terms with the clergy outside of the induction by the governor. Mr. Magowan had just come into the parish, and the vestry sought to make terms with him, offering him a given sum of twenty-five thousand pounds of tobacco, worth about one hundred and sixty pounds currency, together with the parsonage, garden and outhouses on the glebe. The rest of the proceeds from the poll, amounting to about seventeen thousand pounds of tobacco, together with the proceeds of the two glebes, they purposed using upon the church property. Mr. Magowan yielded for the time to the proposition, and entered upon his work. His case was peculiar, and shows what the clergy would have been exposed to under the most favorable circumstances without just such a law as Maryland had. That Mr. Magowan should have been in the parish without induction, surprises us, but the reason doubtless was that there was no Governor in the colony, and that he who acted in the interval had no authority for this office. Governor Sharpe had been recalled in August 1768, and Governor Eden did not enter upon his duties till June, 1769. Within that time therefore the vestries had license, and as in this case, they used it. The vestry had the benefit of this arrangement, however, only for six months, for a letter bearing the date of June twenty-first 1769 was presented by him in August of that year, and he assumed the emoluments as well the authority of rector. The vestry had in the meanwhile proceeded with their plans, tarring "the ruff of the church with tarr and read oaker," and painting the "head of the church three times over with cloud'd blew," covering the "ruff" of their new vestry house with "siprus" shingles, and having new " spike headd gates" and "tarred posts and rales" about the church yard, also causing " Diel post to be sot up." Before presenting his letter let us take up events in their order of time.

Rev. Mr. Adams died October twentieth, 1767, and a few days after we find a document bearing date of October twenty-fourth, which is altogether different from anything seen up to this time. It has a pious guise but is a disguise for conduct as unworthy as usually falls to the lot of a civil officer to conceal. It is also probably different from any letter ever penned by a Governor of Maryland.

MARYLAND Ss.

HORATIO SHARPE, Esq.

Lieutenant governor and ordinary under the Right Honorable, the Lord Proprietary of this province to the Rev. Bennet Allen of Ann Arundel county sendeth greeting:

Whereas, it hath been represented to me that by the decease of the Rev. Mr. Alex. Adams, lately rector of St. James' parrish in Ann Arundel county, the said parish is become vacant, and whereas it is very expedient that some minister of the church of England should reside and be impowered to officiate and administer the sacrament in the said parish until another rector shall be appointed and inducted, I do therefore by these presents grant license and faculty to you, the said Bennet Allen, to officiate as a curate in the said parish, called St. James' parish, and to continue during pleasure, and during such continuance to have, take and receive from the sheriff of Ann Arundell county the whole amount of the thirty per poll as may be due from the taxable inhabitants in the parish aforesaid.

Given under my hand and seal, ect.

It will be observed that this is not a letter of induction, but only the appointment of a curate, and that not where there is a rector, but where there was a vacancy. Also it is the appointment of a curate to serve until a rector shall be appointed, and yet by a contradiction he is to continue curate during pleasure, evidently the curate's own.

The history of the whole matter, as brought out in the letters of governor Sharpe is this. Mr. Allen, though in orders, was a most unworthy companion and favorite of his dissolute lordship. Frederick, the proprietary. In his desire to help his favorite without cost to himself his lordship first laid his commands upon the governor to appoint him to a parish, he to enjoy the emoluments of the same while remaining in England, a curate serving for him. The governor had the courage to tell the proprietary that this would not do, that it would be very ill advised. And so Mr. Allen had to come over to America when he was appointed to St. Anne's, Annapolis. But one parish did not satisfy his needs, and Lord Baltimore urged that he be appointed to two or more; but the Maryland law was against that unless the consent of both parishes could be obtained, such having been a provision made for a case where two weak parishes could neither separately support a rector.

This explains the letter. Governor Sharpe was anxious to please his lordship, but dare not break the law; for the people of Maryland were now exceedingly sensitive against all appearance of prerogative. Mr. Adams' death had for some time been expected, he being a very old man; and as soon as it occurred, knowledge of it was sent to Annapolis, so that within four days, Mr. Allen's papers were issued. St. James' was then worth three hundred pounds. But Gov. Sharpe made a mistake when he thought that by varying the title he might evade the law, and Mr. Allen made a mistake when he supposed the people of St. James' would be satisfied if he appointed a curate while he enjoyed a part of the revenue. His curate was the Rev. Mr. Edmiston, afterwards of St. Anne's, who seems to have been a worthy man if Mr. Eddis' notice refers to him. This scheming on the part of the governor finally brought him and his protegé into trouble. For the people of St. James' objected, and the people of St. Anne's objected, and as Mr. Allen's temper appears to have been belligerant, the tumult waxed warm. He went, in the former parish, to see one of his vestrymen, but the end of the pastoral call was that he was turned out of the house, and with so much emphasis that he felt bound in "honor" to challenge his parishioner to a duel. The challenge was accepted, but of the two, the one not on the ground was Mr. Allen. In Annapolis the feud was as bitter, only it was not settled for some years, when, both Mr. Allen and Mr. Walter Dulaney having gone to England, the latter because of his tory principles, the two met on the duelling ground and Mr. Dulaney was killed.

Mr. Allen's difficulties in St. James' did not, however, make him withdraw; rather he sought to avoid the trouble by resigning St. Anne's and becoming rector of St. James. Governor Sharpe granted this also, but there is no evidence of his having presented his letter of appointment to the parish. Most probably he did not, because on May 27, 1768, we find him inducted in All Saints', Frederick county, the richest living in the colony, being reckoned at five hundred pounds. It is most likely that before he presented his letter to the vestry of St. James' the opportunity was afforded of getting into All

Saints', and hungry for income only, governor Sharpe pleased him by giving him the best the province afforded. But there now could be no peace for him in any Maryland parish. His reputation had gone before him to his new cure, and the antagonism was so intense, and the confusion caused by his appearing so extreme, that he was prevented from reading service. The old Maryland men were very rough, as they were also very ready, and they were just as resolved not to have the welfare of their souls bartered away by the governor's ambition or the lord proprietary's depravity as they were to have their property seized by royal or proprietary presumption.

Governor Sharpe's conduct in this will be a deep blot always upon his reputation in Maryland history. He may have been amiable and generous, as doubtless he was, but he was either cowardly or ambitious, at the same time, and he betrayed the very highest of the prerogatives of his position for his present security. But Nemesis had her dwelling place in his own actions; for when he had tried in vain to satisfy the favorite's desires by betraying the spiritual welfare of the people into his keeping, he finally appointed him agent in charge of his lordship's pecuniary affairs. But that Lord Baltimore did not relish. Mr. Allen might be good enough for the cure of souls, but he was not good enough for handling the revenue, and the governor found too late that in exalting the favorite he was ruining himself. He was recalled in August, 1768.

We have seen the circumstances attending the introduction of Mr. Magowan to the parish.

They were very irregular, but regularity was restored by his letter from governor Eden, June 21, 1769. The letter itself, however, marks an era in Maryland church life. For it runs as no other letter up to this time had run, in this form.

Maryland ss.

Frederick absolute lord and proprietary of the province of Maryland and Avalon, Lord Baron of Baltimore, &c.

To the Rev. Mr. Walter Magowan sendeth greeting:

We do hereby constitute and appoint you, the said Walter Magowan to be rector of the church of St. James' in Ann Arundell county, to have, hold, and enjoy the said church, together with all the rights, profits and advantages whatsoever appertaining to a minister of the said parish, and we do hereby require the church wardens, vestrymen and all other parishioners of the said parrish, to receive, acknowledge and assist you, the said Walter Magowan in all matters relating to the discharge of your functions. Witness our trusty and well beloved Robert Eden, Esq., governor and commander-in-chief in and over the said province, this twenty-first day of June, in the nineteenth year of our dominion, Anno Domini 1769.

Signed by order,

W. SCOTT, Cl. Con.

Robert Eden.

The first thing notable in this is the man who takes this proud title and office to himself For, the last of the Baltimores, he was the most unworthy that had ever succeeded to the name. His moral life was bad, he is described as one of the most licentious of his time. Only in the year 1768 he had been tried for his life, being accused of a most infamous assault upon a female, and though acquitted, he was believed generally to have been guilty. His son and the inheritor of the province, was the fruit of his licentiousness. But not only was he vicious; he was also a most conceited fool, bewailing the fact that God had given him so much genius and so little bodily vigor. His conceit took the form of considering himself learned, and he was fond of displaying his talents in publication. In 1767 he published a book with the title: "A Tour to the East in the Years 1763 and 1764; with Remarks on the City of Constantinople and the Turks; also Select Pieces of Oriential Wit, Poetry and Wisdom," which was described at the time as "no more deserving to be published than his bills on the road for post-horses." He was immensely wealthy, having an income of thirty thousand pounds. He died in 1771.. This is the man that styles himself Frederick, absolute lord, and thinks it meet for him to dispose of, in a princely way, the livings of Maryland and the cure of souls, livings which neither he nor his ancestors had done anything to create, and whose support had never involved him to the amount of a penny. He is the same who expressed his pleasure that the clergy of Maryland should not assemble together for any purpose. He is the one also who inspired his trusty lieutenant, governor Eden, to assume a cold and repulsive manner toward the clergy when they came to petition him concerning the episcopate for the colonies.

But it is not only the man; it is the office also

that he assumes to himself, which is the bestowal
of parishes in his own name which had formerly
been done by his governors. The act of establishment, passed while Maryland was a royal
colony, bestowed that faculty upon the governor;
but Lord Baltimore could justify his pretensions in the matter, not only by the fact that
the governor in the colony was only his agent,
but also by his charter rights which were restored to him in full when the family became
Protestant. As we have seen this question had
been a leading one within the last year or two;
and it was probably to vindicate his rights now
that the form of the letter of induction was
changed. Nevertheless, as far as it indicated a
change in the administration of church affairs it
was a great misfortune. For if the governor
present, with the whole weight of public opinion
about him, and with, at any rate, a knowledge
of the clergy already in the province, could commit blunders, or would settle improper persons
over parishes, how much greater the danger and
how much more hopeless the attempt at discipline,
if he were deprived of all authority and responsibility, and made only the witness of what his
lordship, resident in England, Italy or Constantinople, might do; for his lordship was fond of
travelling. And that this authority in his hands
meant more than a mere form, we have seen in
Mr. Allen's case. All that was necessary was
for him to be aware that a parish was vacant, and
any companion of his revels could secure a presentation from him, and he need never hear of
the protests and indignation of Maryland
citizens. Truly the church was reaching that

last stage when deliverance had to come. American citizenship was too manful to endure such pupilage much longer.

If Mr. Magowan entered upon his duties as rector in times of great disturbance, he certainly did not find them to become less so through the whole period of his rectorship which lasted till 1784. Nor was it only the agitation of the times; it was prevalent largely in his own parish; for some of the most outspoken, and we must also say violent men of the day, were found within the limits of St. James'. And yet, blessed testimony, the church records bear no evidence of such a condition. Church life moved on slowly, church duties were done faithfully; and save that we find the vestry's functions to cease abruptly in 1776, and again later its affairs to be administered by a good many men with a military title, we would not have known from them that there had been any warlike commotion in the land. Mr. Magowan was one of those who took the oath of fidelity and so he was not disturbed during the war. Thus St. James' was blessed above many of the cures of the new state.

The Declaration of Independence, and the disestablishment of the church in consequence, was of course immediately felt by Mr. Magowan, as by all the other rectors in Maryland; for the voluntary contributions of the people were not equal to those formerly enforced for the support of religion. And soon the people became unable to do what they might desire. In consequence of this Mr. Magowan took charge of All Saints', Calvert, in conjunction with St. Jame's, and judging from the large number of marriages he was called on to perform he was the only minister available within a large circuit. The number in 1781 was fourty-four. These afforded him some revenue, and with the two glebes he was at any rate safe from starvation. He thought so apparently himself, for in 1780 he married, the lady being Elizabeth Harrison, and the officiating minister, Mr. Hanna, from north of the Severn. He was the fourth minister who finished his earthly labors while in the parish.

But however much the affairs of the province and of the church might be disturbed previous to 1776, the vestry did not fail to attend to their duties. They held their meetings, required the presence of each other even to the point of laying a fine upon absentees of ten shillings currency "besides what is directed by law." The current needs also were jealously looked into among which we find the unusual item that Mr. Magowan was paid four pounds for keeping the surplice and plate two years, a payment you hardly know how to appreciate. He was paid for the same again the next year, showing it was no accident. Upon its face it would appear that there was great anxiety on the parson's part to secure all the revenue possible for however slight a service, and that the church was an employer to serve rather than a cure of souls to foster. It will be remembered that probably the most violent and long continued struggle the church had ever had with the colony about clerical salaries, was now raging. The consequence was of necessity jealousy on the part of the parsons, and a willingness to obtain for themselves all the revenue possible. That they were sometimes betrayed into littleness was only to be expected. The vestry also at this time had abundant means, nearly sixteen thousand pounds of tobacco being in the hands of one man, bought at the high price of twenty-seven shillings and six pence per hundred. It had also the attendant difficulties necessarialy resulting from such business, with threats to sue for recovery.

The church ceased to exist as an establishment November 3d, 1776, by the passage of the Declaration of Rights. Two days afterwards the vestry came together and in a most business like way proceeded to settle up its affairs, paying off all outstanding obligations. The change had evidently been looked forward to and provided for. It was known to have become necessary. The revolution that was taking place was by the people in their freedom and sovereignty, and of necessity everything that had its rise or existence in partial views of right and liberty had to be done away. Property as well as life was sacred. This was the foundation of the American system as now developing, and so a state church, which could only be the fruit of partial legislation, had to cease. This was felt all over America. It was particularly felt in Maryland where some of the sturdiest blows against prerogative had within the few last years been given by a representative of the great disfranchised class, the Roman Catholics, Charles Carroll of Carrollton being the man. The vestry had felt and known this, and so as soon as a messenger could repeat to them the action of the convention they were ready as a corporation to adjust their record and cease to be. Their last act was to give an order to the rector on the sheriff for the amount of the assessment by him collected.

But though they took things so philosophically, yet doubtless all those who loved the church must have been filled with forebodings; for not only was a great change wrought in going from an enforced to a voluntary system for support, which is always doubtful, but this was done when the air was filled with the sound of war, and when the certain prostration of commerce was to bring to every plantation in Maryland narrow means if not financial distress. The number of polls in 1772 was fourteen hundred and sixty-five, about three times what it had been in 1700, and the revenue from this and the glebes had been abundant, probably more than it has ever been since. This abundant provision had now to be relinquished, and what was to be the result no one knew. And let us not imagine it was the parson only who had apprehensions. The old parish had long since become the admiration and love of the people. The church was the church of their fathers and blessed associations had long since clung around it, as they have continued to this day. Besides, what would become of their souls' interests if the doors of the sanctuary should be closed? The word and sacraments, how could they do without them? These thoughts, doubtless, troubled them, but nevertheless they had to descend into the darkness. But blessed above many in the land, the doors never were closed, God's minister never was silent, and after a brief interval we find the corporation showing life again and gathering its resources for the perpetuation of the church's work.

CHAPTER XVIII.

1776—1792.

Upon her disestablishment the church in Maryland found herself in the midst of wholly unpropitious circumstances. To brave those circumstances and to rise triumphant above them, was now her duty, and she was not found incapable. At first she was content simply to exist, her existence and her rights preserved. Energy it was hardly possible for her to show when the public mind was so engrossed in the great war and all resources were reduced to the lowest point. For the agriculturists of Maryland, who were the great body of her people, suffered probably more than most of the other colonies, seeing that tobacco, Maryland's great staple, was cut off from a market, and the people had to change their whole style of husbandry. Most of the churches were kept open, though with the small salaries and the reduced number of active ministers, a clergyman often had to serve several parishes. Some of the churches were not kept open, but owing to local circumstances, the carelessness or the poverty of the people, were allowed to go to ruin, to be trespassed upon and torn to pieces either by the wanton wickedness or the sacriligious spirit of the community. Where such was the sad misfortune of the church it required many years to repair the evil and open the sacred house again for prayer and praise. In almost all instances, however, if not in all, this has been done ; for there are but few old ruins in Maryland to mark spots from which the church has had to recede. The church in Maryland had for too many years been part of the social fabric to allow it an easy death, and when times brightened men began to look up and God answered their prayers ; and old dismantled and desecrated buildings were consecrated anew.

As early as April, 1778, within eighteen months of the passage of the Bill of Rights, we find the people in St. James' parish coming together, in "a meeting of freemen" to choose persons to act as vestrymen, and in all probability the records of other parishes would show the same ; for where the church was kept open during the war it would soon be found essential to have some persons to attend to its affairs and to be custodians of its property. They do not seem to have been acting under any law, but rather of their own will. Nor was any time appointed during which those elected were to serve. They also immediately went to work to secure funds for the necessary expenses of the church, and judging from the list returned Nov. 15th, 1779, their efforts met with a willing response from the people, for at that time sixty-eight persons were represented as subscribing different sums. In 1781 however, the number of subscribers was one hundred and fifty-five, showing a very general disposition to sustain the church. The net they cast was pretty large, to catch all manner of fish, none being allowed to escape by reason of its size ; for the heading to the list in 1779 reads: Whereas no act has hitherto been made for the support of the clergy of the church of England by the legislature of this state, we the subscribers do therefore bind and oblige ourselves, our heirs, executors, or administrators, to pay unto the vestry of the aforesaid parish (St. James) or their order, the sum of money, or quantity of tobacco, wheat, corn, rye, oats, peas or beans annexed to our respective names, on or before the first day of Dec. 1780, to be applied by said vestry towards employing a clergyman to officiate in said parish for one year from the date hereof, and to defray other necessary expenses of said parish." Nobody, however, seems to have contributed anything except money and tobacco, of which there evidently there was still much raised. Among the vestrymen chosen in 1778, was the Rev. Walter Magowan, his holding of the parish for the last eighteen months being apparently by common consent. The spirit of the old institution was also evidently still hanging about them, for the act of 1779, entitled an act for the establishment of select vestries, did not admit the rector of the parish into this body. This act was passed in the March session of this year, and was as liberal towards the church as it could well be , for the church itself had by no means been educated up to the expectation or desire of liberal things such as are now looked upon as essential in her relations with the state. The preamble to the act was a follows: "Whereas it is thought expedient and necessary that select vestries be chosen in every parish within the state for the preservation of the churches and for the taking care of glebe lands and other purposes tending to the happiness and welfare of the state." And according to the first section the number of the vestrymen was to be seven, to be elected by persons contributing to the support of the parish, and who were qualified to vote for members of the assembly. The members elect, also, were to take the following oath in addition to that of faithfulness in their office: I. A. B. do swear that I do not hold myself bound to yield any allegiance or obedience to the King of Great Britain, his heirs or successors, and that I will be true and faithful to the state of Maryland, and will, to the utmost of my power, support, maintain, and defend the freedom and independence thereof, and the government as it is now established, against all open enemies and secret traitorous conspiracies, attempts or combinations against this state or the government thereof which may come to my knowledge: So help me God." Such an oath was afterwards continued under the vestry act of 1798, only it was so modified as to read: "I do swear that I do not hold myself bound in allegiance to the King of Great Britain, and that I will be faithful and bear true allegiance to the state of Maryland." This oath continued to be administered to vestrymen for more than fifty years after the declaration of American independence.

Among the other features of the law of 1779 was one requiring, as under the old system, a table of marriages to be set up in the churches; and to ensure care and attention on the part of the people to their church duties, the vestry was required to meet monthly, fines being imposed for absence. Also if any person, a member of the church, and possessing the qualifications named for a vestryman, should refuse, upon election to serve, unless he had sufficient excuse to allege, he was fined twenty pounds currency, and half that amount was imposed upon any warden who in like circumstances, refused to bear the burdens of office. And this is still the law in Maryland by the twenty-sixth article of the vestry act ; only the fines are ten and twenty dollars instead of ten and twenty pounds. Such fines also are recoverable before any justice of the peace. That any attempt should be made now to collect such fines no one imagines, for it would be recognized not only as an act of extreme folly, but also as violating that principle of free-will offering to God for his church's sake which everybody now recognizes as the true root of the church's prosperity. And the sentiment is that anyone that could only thus be constrained to be a vestryman, would only be a hindrance and a curse within that body. The flavor of old things still pervaded the church's new relations ; neither the church nor the state could understand how true and entire their separation had been. All through this period the consciousness was expressed, not only that the church was dependent upon the state for protection in temporal things, but that it was for the highest profit of the state that in every legitimate way religion should be fostered. It was a mutual partnership for mutual support. Since that day both church and state have entered upon larger ideas. The oath of faithfulness to the state of Maryland has been lost in the grander idea of fealty to the general government, and the church in Maryland, while preserving her diocesan autonomy in many things, is a part of the church of America with a community of interests embracing the whole land.

The act for the establishment of select vestries shows the kindest feeling on the part of the state authorities towards the church, and along with the recognition of the principles of the declaration of rights, the utmost desire to promote her welfare. And well might it be so, for at that time almost all the intelligence and influence of the state were found in the body called the church of England. For the great inroads, chiefly by Methodism, upon the church had hardly then begun, and everywhere care and affection were felt for the only known mother that had nourished the people, preaching the word, administering the bread of life, ministering in the hours both of joy and sorrow in the homes. When the inroads were made they were successful chiefly among the poor, but at this time they also were loyal. The great subscription list of 1781, when one hundred and fifty-five persons combined in the one parish given to support the ministry, very many of them poor and of the humblest walks of life, as shown by their gifts as well as by their names, is an instance and proof of this. Well, therefore, might the feeling of the legislature be kind, for it represented only the common feeling.

Under this act the vestries were immediately reorganized, save where both spiritual and pecuniary destitution abounded. It gave the church a position again, and set the machinery in motion. Seven vestrymen were called for and two church wardens; but care was taken to exclude the rector from a seat, probably owing to the old jealousies of the parson on account of his former impregnable position. Care was now taken and preserved through many years, that he should not be able to defy the will of the people and stay on. This was accomplished by making him only an employe, which was attained by excluding him from the vestry whose acts would thus be independent of him, by retaining the purse strings in their own hands, and by making agreements only for short terms. This exclusion of the minister continued till 1790, when by the action of a church convention, held in Easton, it was recommended that "the minister and church wardens be joined with the vestry in transacting church business which may come before them." The interposition of the minister had been found so far necessary, and he had ceased to be the mere hireling for certain purposes. He was part of the institution. An extract from the records of one parish, St. James', under this date is interesting. The minister entering the vestry, had laid before it the constitution and canons both of the general convention and also of the church in Maryland for consideration, of which the vestry expressed its hearty approval, save of one feature, that the diocesan constitution restrained the convention from choosing more than one bishop. This the vestry regarded as a mistake, thinking that one could not serve the whole state. But the trouble was that the convention only purposed to bestow jurisdiction on its bishops, and for his daily bread he was to provide as he could, by his private fortune or by his salary as a parish minister. Therefore they could have what opinions they might choose. The support of twenty bishops would be no more than the support of one, for that was nothing. Opinions, therefore, were cheap. It will be remembered that in 1814 Maryland did elect a suffragan bishop.

We have seen that the declaration of rights of 1776, recognized the principle that the citizens of the commonwealth might be taxed for the support of religion. In the year 1780, in the hour of her distress, the church remembered this and sought to have her needs provided for by a law framed upon that principle. This was at a meeting of the clergy and laity held in Chestertown when the form of a petition was drawn up to be sent around to the various parishes of the state, that being thus numerously signed it might have the needed weight. The form of the petition was "That an act may be passed agreeably to the aforesaid declaration of rights, for the support of public religion by an equal assessment and laws, and also to enable the vestry and church wardens of this parish by rates on the pews from time to time, or otherwise, as your wisdom shall think fit, to repair and uphold the church and chapel and the church yard and burying ground of the same." Surely a striking instance of the acceptance of a false position, a church born to new and nobler relations, but still in swaddling bands: for the church proposed to leave it to the "wisdom" of the legislators, who were of all creeds as well as of none, to say what system, if any, she should pursue in raising funds from her children for her support. From the circumstances of the times, when the time, attention and resources of the people were absorbed by the war, this effort was perceived to be hopeless, and so was not prosecuted. Also it may have begun to dawn upon the minds of its favorers as an incongruity that one "society" as even church people called the church at the time, should appeal for a tax upon christians of every name, and also it may have begun to be perceived that a tax at all for religion under the new order of affairs and the broad liberty of the new commonwealth, was out of place. The ground of appeal, however, was not only the maintenance of religion; though church representatives could never ignore that chief consideration; but in their petition the vestries dwelt strongly upon the fact, "That where religion is left to mourn and droop her head, while her sacred ordinances are unsupported, and vice and immorality gain ground, even war itself will be but feebly carried on, patriotism will lose its animating principle, corruption will win its way from the lowest to the highest places, distress will soon pervade every public measure, our graveyards, the monuments of the piety of our ancestors, running to ruin, will become the reproach of their posterity. Nay, more, the great and glorious fabric of public happiness, which we are striving to build up and cement with an immensity of blood and treasure, might be in danger of tumbling into the dust as wanting the stronger cement of virtue and religion, or perhaps would fall an easy prey to some haughty invader." To avert such terrible consequences churchmen were asked to petition the legislature for the tax, and from various parts of the state petitions were sent up. And, doubtless, religion was depressed, and immorality in a degree did flourish in consequence; but, fortunately, religion was delivered by a higher and better power than a state tax, with an enfranchisement that was far more noble and enduring. The church flourishes best when she does not look to the assistance, whether willing or unwilling, of "the sordid and the selfish, the licentious and profane" whom it was hoped by this means to compel. The measure though failing in 1782 was renewed again in 1783, being fostered by the action of Governor Paca who brought the proposition before the assembly. The church regarded the establishment of peace and the assured position of the country among the nations of the earth as a fit occasion for granting state aid. But though so powerfully supported, again the measure came to nothing. Though such longing eyes looked out, and such hopeful hands were in vain extended, yet all of the clergy were not like that brother who in 1784 refused to attend a church convention because it had not been summoned by state authority.

Through all this time the parishes were struggling to sustain themselves; and with sufficient difficulty to please everyone who might have remembered with aversion their abundance in other days. The common recourse was to join several parishes together, with service on different Sundays; an unfortunate necessity wherever it prevails, as it still does in many places. For either loyalty is wounded in our members going off to other houses of worship on the intervening Sundays, or devotion is cooled by their idling at home. But few have the gace to occupy the day for their spiritual profit in their closets.

Among the parishes that were compelled to have recourse to this means for support was St. James', and by the advice of the vestry we find the rector assuming to his care All Saints, Calvert Co   Mr. Magowan, who died in 1784, was at that time performing this double duty, and his successor, the Rev. Dr. Thos. John Claggett, who became rector in 1786, Aug. 1st, gave his care and attention to the same extensive field. This gentleman who, while still rector of St. James in 1792, was elected to the episcopate of Maryland, had previously held various parishes, on all of which he doubtless made a strong impression. For he was a man of marked force of character, and along with his learning, he was exact and business like in his engagements and transactions; one of those men that in a crisis prove of permanent and enduring value to the enterprise in which they are engaged. So as afterwards in diocesan matters, it was now in parochial concerns. Everything was done decently and in order; but besides he was able to enkindle in the parish he occupied for the six years after 1786, a deep interest in all general church affairs, making that parish to be a fair representative of the best parochial life of the day.

He was first chosen for three years, and was afterwards reelected three several times for one year each, probably by his own preference for such a short term. This election for a limited term was then the universal custom, begotten doubtless by the unfortunate experience of the colonial times when a man inducted could defy all authority to remove him. The act of 1779 provided for the election of rectors for limited terms, as well as does that of 1798 still in force. The prevalence of the contrary custom is the result of the fact that the clergy can in the vast majority of cases, be trusted; that the old method of electing annually took away from the independence and selfrespect of the minister, who became so far an annual applicant for the suffrage of the people, the question of his tenure entering into every election of vestrymen; and and also, that the highest welfare of the parish is promoted by the long continued residence of the pastor.

But if the people provided for their own protection, the clergy in some instances were watchful to provide for theirs, and could not be induced to enter upon the duties of a rectorship until they had every guarantee that their salary was well secured; for there were a good many promises to pay which were never realized by the parsons. Dr. Claggett was one of this careful sort, and before he would enter upon the rectorship, we find this among the parish records: "Ordered that the Register write to Mr. Thomas John Claggett informing him that the following gentlemen of the vestry, viz: Mr. John Hall, Mr. Ezekiel Gott, Mr. Benjamin Burgess, Capt. William Weems, and one private gentleman, Maj. Richard Chew, had left their obligations with the Register which obligations are to be delivered to the said Claggett on his obligating himself to the vestry for his performance for three years. The other gentilemen of the vestry promise on their honour that they will do everything in their power to make up the remaining part of the sallery."

In consequence of this communication, the following agreement was drawn up and signed : "St. James parish, July 21st, 1786, at a vestry met and held in the vestry room of the said parish by the vestrymen thereunto legally authorized and appointed on the day and year above written, present Col. John Weems, John Hall, Ezekiel Gott, Richard Harrison, Benjamin Burgess, Capt. Wm. Weems, and Zechariah Childs, church warden. The Rev. Doct. Thomas John Claggett appears and agrees to officiate in the aforesaid parish church every other sabbath and to perform all the accustomed duties of the said parish for three years unless prevented by sickness or other unforseen casualty.

For and in consideration of the above services the vestry do hereby license, induct, constitute and appoint him, the said Thomas John Claggett (Doc. in Divinity) rector of the said parish, and give him the free use and enjoyment of all and every the glebes and their appurtenances, together with the exclusive right to the pulpit in the parish church, and all other privileges, immunities and advantages which any minister of this parish ought to enjoy: This agreement to continue and be in full force for and during the term of three years, to commence from the first day of August, 1786, unless death, sickness or any other unforseen accident should cause the said Claggett to vacate the parish, and in that case only it shall be null and void."

To this writing is appended the name of Dr. Claggett only. Why, as it was a letter of induction and appointment his name only was signed does not appear. The spirit of the old times had evidently not departed, and while parson and people could respect and love each other, as they evidently did, yet they had great confidence mutually that business could not be done in too regular and careful a way,—an example it would be well for both clergy and vestries now to follow more frequently than they do. In consequence of this particularity Dr. Claggett's rectorship was peaceful throughout and he was able to wield a large power for usefulness. Also he was able to stimulate the people to give great attention to the general affairs of the church both in the diocese and also in the country at large. Fortunately he found men in the vestry who had sufficient intelligence and devotion to the church to make them take great interest. He was doubtless in congenial company, and being a resident in the parish he had constant opportunities to make his influence permanent. How much St. James' parish owes to his residence in it at this time it would be impossible to say.

One of the first subjects brought to the consideration of the churchmen of Maryland in those days was the rights, inherent and necessary, that belonged to the church. This question had been first agitated in 1783 when it had been proposed in the legislature of the state to appoint ordainers for the ministry; a strong testimony of the attachment of the people to the former establishment, along with a marvelous ignorance of the very first principle of its true position. This proposition was of course immediately and successfully resisted by the church clergy, one of whom was publicly heard before the house upon the measure. The fact that such a proposition could be made, however, alarmed the church and so at a meeting of a convention held at Anaapolis in August in the year above given "Certain fundamental Rights and Liberties of the Protestant Episcopal Church of Maryland" were distinctly declared. This convention it will also be remembered, elected Dr. William Smith to the Episcopate, though for certain reasons he was never consecrated. This declaration, however, of rights and liberties was not at that time submitted to the vestries, because though the convention that passed it was regarded as valid, yet things were still in an inchoate condition. In 1788 there a was general review of past action and this Declaration along with certain other completed acts, as canons and rules were sent down, and all the parishes were called on to earnestly consider them. As they embraced eminent principles it was a most excellent means of instructing the people. These rights and liberties which it was felt to be necessary to proclaim to the world, but especially to the state of Maryland under whose "constitution and form of government" the church was existing, were enumerated as follows:

1st. We consider it as the undoubted right of the said Protestant Episcopal Church, in common with other christian churches under the American revolution, to complete and preserve herself as an entire church agreeably to her ancient usages and professions, and to have the full enjoyment and free exercise of those purely spiritual powers which are essential to the being of every church or congregation of the faithful, and which, being derived only from Christ and his apostles, are to be maintained independent of every foreign or other jurisdiction so far as may be consistant with the civil rights of society.

2nd. That ever since the reformation it hath been the received doctrine of the church whereof we are members, (and which by the constitution of this state is entitled to the perpetual enjoyment of certain property and rights under the denomination of the church of England) that there be these three orders of ministers in Christ's Church, Bishops, Priests and Deacons; and that an Episcopal ordination and commission are necessary to the valid administration of the sacraments and the due exercise of the ministerial function in the said church.

3d. That without calling in question the rights, modes and forms of any other christian church or societies, or wishing the least contest with them on that subject, we consider and declare it to be an essential right of the said Protestant Episcopal church to have and enjoy the continuance of the said three orders of ministers so far as concerns matters purely spiritual, and that no persons in the character of ministers, except such as are in the commission of the said church, and duly called to the ministry by regular Episcopal ordination, can or ought to be admitted into or enjoy, any of the churches, chapels, glebes, or other property formerly belonging to the church of England in this state, and which by the constitution and form of Government is secured to the said church forever, by whatever name the said church or her superior order of ministers may in future be denominated.

4th. That as it is the right so it will be the duty of the said church, when duly organized, constituted and represented in a synod or convention of the different orders of her ministry and people, to revise her liturgy, forms of prayer, and public worship in order to adapt the same to the late Revolution and other local circumstances of America; which it is humbly conceived, may and will be done without any other or farther departure from the venerable order and beautiful forms of worship from whence we sprang, than may be found expedient in the change of our situation from a daughter to a sister church."

This copy is taken from the books of St. James parish, on which the vestry had had it spread because it was regarded as of such great importance. That the document was important, is evident from the fact that after an interval of five years from its passage it was thought advisable to publish it again a second time. And it was important because, knowing Episcopacy only as it existed in England where immense prerogatives were enjoyed by the Episcopal order, and where the lord bishops had almost always been on the side of arbitrary government and had used their power for the repression of the liberties of the people, the citizens of America from one end of the country to the other, stood in dread of it; so that the possibility of the institution of Episcopacy was one of the chief causes leading to the Revolution. The order as represented in the persons and office of Bishops

Seabury, White or Claggett, was something of which the American mind had up to this time formed no idea. The church in South Carolina, it will be remembered, was glad to be enrolled among the dioceses of the land, only it did not want a Bishop.

It was against this prejudice, therefore, at this time the church in Maryland was providing for herself. She was determined to secure the episcopate and had taken the first step in 1783, she dreaded to have her altars invaded, as well as her property possessed by those whom she could not look upon as duly ordained. She feared those proposed to be appointed by the state as ordainers to the ministry, and she dreaded lest the body of enemies who surrounded her and whom she had in other days done little to conciliate, should be able to seize on some lapse of hers, as the change of her name, or the change of her liturgy, to deprive her of the possession of her churches, chapels, or other devout benefactions of her children in other days for the support of her ministry. How far there was reason for that fear is questionable. With her declaration, however, her rights were preserved; how far it was by it we do not know. Certainly the state of Maryland looked with favor on the church in Maryland, as was proven when the legislature admitted a clergyman to argue a church question before it and then decided according to his argument. That the great powerful organization of 1776 should have been compelled in 1783 to put forth such a document suggests a contrast that excites our sympathies. It was a change, however, out of which noble fruits were in time to grow. Her hesitation about her name and that of "her superior order of ministers" which was expressed in 1783, was to be forgotten in the church's strongly pronounced views and claims of the days to come.

If the church, however, was so bold in declaring her rights and liberties she was not ready to be quite so bold in acting up to her declaration; for in 1783 we find her appealing to the legislature of the state for privilege to change her name and adapt her liturgy as well as to secure for herself the means of perpetuating her ministry. To make this appeal may have been partly the result of former training and partly fear of jeopardizing her property secured to her as the church of England. But whatever the cause, the fact was felt by others to be unnecessary, and the attempt was looked upon with jealousy as in some way an endeavor to secure state recognition for the church. The contest that arose was bitter, but the appeal of the church was favorably received by the assembly. This was in May, and it was in the August following that the declaration of liberties was made and the Rev. Dr. William Smith elected to the Episcopate.

Another document of great interest issued at this time was a declaration of "certain fundamental principles of the Protestant Episcopal Church of Maryland, &c." In it the church labored to minimize her positions, to assert as little as was possible; these principles being rather as postulates which were to be the basis of the legislation which she saw to be necessary, and which she would as soon as might be enact. It will be remembered that the dioceses had at first to act for themselves, and legislation was necessary in them which was afterwards delegated to the General Convention; also in the earlier conventions of Maryland down to and including those of 1783, only clergy had sat. In 1784 lay delegates were present, and their approval became neceszary to all acts passed. It was at this time this declaration of "certain fundamental principles" was made to regulate and control the relations of the various orders in the church among themselves. These principles are as follows:

"1st. None of the orders of the clergy, whether Bishops, Priests or Deacons, who may be under the necessity of obtaining ordination in any foreign state with a view to officiate or settle in this state, shall, at the time of their ordination, or at any time afterwards, take or subscribe any obligation of obedience, civil or canonical, to any foreign power or authority whatsoever, nor be admissible into the ministry of this church if such obligation have been taken for a settlement in any foreign country, without renouncing the same by taking the oaths required by law, as a test of allegiance to this state.

"2nd. According to what we conceive to be true apostolic institution, the duty and office of a Bishop differs in nothing from that of other priests except in the power of ordination and confirmation, and in the right of precedency in ecclesiastical meetings or synods, and shall accordingly be so exercised in this church; the duty and office of Priests and Deacons to remain as heretofore; and if any further distinctions and regulations in the different orders of the ministry should afterwards be found necessary for the good government of the church, the same shall be made and established by the joint voice and authority of a representative body of clergy and laity at future ecclesiastical synods or conventions.

"3d. This third section is intended to define or discriminate some of the separate rights and powers of the clergy and was proposed and agreed to as follows, viz.: that the clergy should be deemed adequate judges of the ministerial commission and authority which is necessary to the due administration of the ordinances of religion in their own church, and of the literary, moral and religious qualities and abilities of persons fit to be nominated and appointed to the different orders of the ministry. But the approving and receiving of such persons to any particular cure, duty or parish when so nominated, appointed, set apart, consecrated and ordained, is in the people who are to support them and to receive the benefit of their ministry."

These principles were the outgrowth of the time, and have all been more or less modified as the feelings and circumstances of those days have changed. For the church feared, and doubtless with reason, that its every act and position were watched with jealousy, a perfectly legitimate state of mind when we remember the old times before the Revolution just closed, and what political position so many of the clergy had assumed during the war. So the first principle in regard to allegiance to any foreign power. Some of the clergy on the breaking out of hostilities or before, had gone back to England, but many had simply surrendered their parishes and discontinued their ministry. The whole body, was therefore under suspicion. Also the infant state was exceedingly sensitive, and did not yet know whom to trust, and consequently the oath of allegiance continued for many years to be generally imposed. Also, various persons, a number from Maryland, were going abroad for ordination, and it was doubtful what they would have to submit to if they would succeed.

For these reasons this principle was enunciated; but as time has since gone on the postulate has been so far modified or ignored as that not only is such oath of allegiance no longer required, but citizens of a foreign state are found in some instances in possession of parishes. Even the vestry act of 1798 did not embody this principle though the oath was required of persons elected vestrymen.

And so in regard to the second proposition, that according to "true apostolic institution the duty and office of a bishop differs in nothing from that of other priests except in the power of ordination and confirmation, and in the right of precedency in ecclesiastical meetings or synods, and shall accordingly be so exercised in this church." This was an overwhelming renunciation of that scheme of Episcopal prerogative which was such a bug-bear in the American mind. It is denied that they are a separate order, but are associated with "other priests," to whom only certain additional functions have been assigned. There are no rights of their order that place them outside of or above the law. There are no fatherly prerogatives by which either priests or people become to them as children. The right to ordain and confirm, and precedency in synods are theirs—nothing more. A wonderful contrast with the functions of their order as exercised by his Lordship, Archbishop Laud, who stood out in the American mind as the embodiment of ecclesiastical enormity, though only the strong representative of his class and order.

But a Bishop is a good deal more than such a functionary as our fathers would have made him. Americans are still right jealous of any "prerogatives" that a bishop may be disposed to assert, and our wisest bishops are very chary of asserting such, but he is the father among his people: his influence is powerful in his diocese ; according as he expresses desires, preferences or intentions will the policy of his diocese become; while his animadversions and rebukes, whether against men or measures will be dreaded. The office has been found of too lofty an origin and its necessary functions too high and holy to allow our fathers' "fundamental principle" to place cramping limitations upon it.

The third principle was also an adaptation, though from a different standpoint; for while the other principles were for the purpose, in large measure, of conciliating the people, this was for the purpose of defending the rights of the clergy in a point where those rights were threatened. And so its object as stated: "to define or discriminate some of the separate rights and powers of the clergy." Formerly under the establishment the laity had nothing to do but accept the rector appointed to their parish and make the best of him. Afterwards, towards the close of the Revolution, as we have seen, the laity, as assembled in the state legislature, considered the proposition of appointing ordainers to the ministry. The clergy, therefore, in 1784 felt that right views concerning their prerogatives were in danger, and so this principle. They would discriminate or define their separate rights and powers. The rights of the laity were of course recognized, that it was for them to receive or not any minister into a parish. But they claimed as their own the right to determine upon " the ministerial commission and authority which is necessary to the due administration of the ordinances of religion in their own church, and of the literary, moral, and religious qualities and abilities of persons fit to be nominated to the different orders of the ministry." They insisted that that power belonged to them, as being by divine right custodians of their own order. And the laity represented in the convention, recognized the principle as sound, and it is one that has controlled the church in Maryland from that day to this; though for a while, in the enactment of canons at this time it would appear that this exclusive right of the clergy over their own order was allowed to fall into abeyance.

It will be remembered that in Connecticut, and particularly in the person of Bishop Seabury, there was an indisposition to admit the laity into church conventions, nor was it a thing which English clergymen were familiar with—the direct influence of the laity ceasing with their power in parliament. Such admission, however, was necesssary in America, and was very soon universally recognized. But Maryland claims the principle and acts on it, that the clergy have entire right over their own order, and so she alone, with Connecticut, has a standing committee composed entirely of clergymen, because one of the chief functions of that standing committee is to pass upon "the literary, moral and religious qualities and abilities of persons to be nominated and appointed to the different orders of the ministry." Also although the laws under which that committee are to act, are passed by a convention composed of both clergy and laity, yet the principle is saved and exemplified by the large discretion that is placed in the hands of the members of that committee. And churchmen are fighting against their true principles when they attempt to limit the freedom of that discretion. Such a committee should have "power" entrusted to it outside and above all conventions, vestries and all other bodies wherein laymen may sit. So only can we be true to this fundamental principle.

But Maryland shows her consistency with this principle in another of her acts, her ecclesiastical court. She was not always consistent, as we shall see presently, but right thinking attained its end when that court was instituted and made to consist only of clergymen. This was a point that Bishop Seabury was earnest for, that the right of trial of clergymen should be only in the hands of the clergy, the power of deprival where the power of ordination rests, and Maryland reached it after a while; because true church principles as such have been at the root of Maryland action. It is observable that the two dioceses that have been strictest in their adherence to this "fundamental principle" are the two whose ratio of communicants to the population today stands the highest.

Another point insisted on at this time was that there should be annual meetings of the convention, a symbol and manifestation of power that must have, to the clergy of that convention in 1784, contrasted most agreeably with the time when the word of a dissolute lordling could forbid their meeting together for God's work. And yet only eight years had intervened! Truly it was freedom!

One of the first thoughts of the church in Maryland after the enunciation of her rights and principles, was the question of discipline, the power to administer which having been the great demand from the beginning. The many attempts that had been made to secure some effective agency for this purpose will here be remembered, attempts that on account of the jealousy of one or other party, had always proven abortive, the church rejecting the mixed court that the state would erect, and the state and the people refusing to allow a Bishop or the delegation of sufficient power to a commissary. Now the church had the power herself, and by a marvelous inconsistency she embodied the principle in her legislation that she had always contended against, and which was in direct contravention of her own above recorded principles. For as Bishop Seabury stated, the power of deprival can only be lodged legitimately in the hands that have the power of ordination, which is what the church in Maryland had always said, when contending against a mixed court. They wanted a Bishop for discipline as the only legitimate and effective means.

And yet one of the first acts finally passed upon in 1788, entitled "Additional constitutions or rules respecting the discipline and government of the Protestant Episcopal church in Maryland," sets out with the statement that the "General Convention of this church (in Maryland) consisting of the different orders of the clergy and laity duly represented, shall have the general cognizance of all affairs necessary to the discipline and good government of the church, including particularly the power and authority necessary for reclaiming or excluding from church privileges scandalous members, whether lay or clerical, and all jurisdiction with regard to offenders, the power of suspending or dismissing clergymen of all orders from the exercise of their ministry in the church."

Also by the second of these constitutions it was appointed, that "Future conventions shall frame and establish rules or canons for receiving complaints, and shall annually appoint a committee consisting of an equal number of clergy and laity, (including the Bishop when there shall be one duly consecrated among the number of the clergy) which committee shall have standing authority, government, and jurisdiction (agreeable to such rules as may be given for that purpose) in all matters respecting the discipline and government of the church that may arise or be necessary to be proceeded upon during the recess or adjournment of general conventions." This term "general convention" is probably used as in contradistinction from the meetings of the superintending and outstanding committees, each of which was composed, but especially the latter, of a large number of persons.

For agreeably to the above provision, by the fourth of the rules of 1788, there was ordered "A standing committee consisting of five clergymen and the like number of laymen, of each shore, the clerical members to be chosen by the clergy and the lay members by the laity, in annual convention. Their duty shall be to correspond with like committees throughout the states and execute the authority given them by the second additional constitution as above inserted." By the ninth and tenth rules also, we have the method of proceeding: "Disorderly, scandalous and immoral conduct, neglect of duty or a disregard to the canons or rules of the church, are offences for which a clergyman may be brought to trial; to which end application shall be made by the accuser to the president for the time being, who shall without delay call together the standing committee to meet at a convenient place on the shore where the accused person resides; a majority of whom, both as to clerical and lay members, shall have authority to inquire into the charge or charges in the presence of both parties, and having heard the evidence, shall proceed to state and report the facts to the next convention, who having heard whatever may be offered by either of the parties in further evidence, shall proceed to pronounce such sentence as they may think the offence deserves; provided that no sentence exceed reproof, suspension or dismission; and that if any accusation is brought against the president, application may be made by the accuser to one clerical and lay member of the standing committee, who shall have the same powers of calling the committee which are hereby given to the president in other cases."

"No vestryman shall sit on the examination or trial of a minister belonging to the parish where such vestryman resides. Complaints against a clergyman shall be received from the vestry of the parish where he officiates, and from no other person or persons whatsoever. They shall be signed by a majority of the vestry and church wardens, without which no complaints shall be received, &c., &c."

Into such loose views of the true relations of the church and her clergy had Maryland at that time come. What was the cause we do not know, how far the clergy had become derelict, how far there were crying evils abroad, how far they were merely bowing to the jealousies of the laity who dreaded an exercise of inherent prerogative in any class, or how far they were providing for a state of things that did not exist. Certainly however, the law was not found to work well. It did not bring the clergy to trial, so that Bishop Claggett had bitterly to bewail the condition of things in some instances where the vestry would not institute proceedings. Vestrymen were known to refuse to complain against their pastors, whatever grievance they thought they were enduring. The law was erroneous in fact also, for it will be found that the clergy are more jealous for the uprightness of their order than the laity are. These will gossip about clerical delinquences, but go no further; while the clergy feel every delinquency a stain on their holy order that ought to be removed, however long suffering they may feel disposed to be.

A superintending committee was at the same time appointed, five members for each shore, to whom the general duty of supervision of the church in the diocese was committed. They were to visit the parishes, dividing them amongst themselves. Also they had charge of candidates for orders, to ascertain their fitness. Also to them was assigned the duty of receiving clergymen entering the diocese, and no vestry or congregation could receive any minister unless he was able to present the testimonial from the superintending committee of their shore, that he had conformed to the law.

This was the provisional arrangement of things in Maryland as finally instituted in 1788, and with all its faultiness it was effective to tide the "society" over its then depressed condition. There was not a great deal of backbone then displayed in various quarters; the sturdiness of Bishop Seabury was not a general property, as is seen in the provisional arrangement suggested by Doctor, afterwards Bishop White. This arrangement which he advanced in his pamphlet of 1782, "The case of the Episcopal Church considered" in which an episcopal Church without episcopacy was thought for the time being available, was something that found reponse in various quarters. "Ordainers for the ministry," were proposed in Maryland, and South Carolina wanted the Episcopal Church without a Bishop. Nowhere did the church thoroughly understand herself or know her true position, save maybe in

New England and New York where the clergy had hold on more vigorous ideas. Everywhere, however, she was working towards a knowledge of her true self which was reached clearly after many days. May the Almighty, her Lord, ever preserve her in this knowlege.

Turning now briefly to parochial affairs, there are a few things to note before we close our pages. One of these is the fact that this is the time when the fine parish libraries of Maryland, not always extensive in numbers, but excellent in quality, began to be scattered. Efforts were made to recover them, but failed, and they were lost one by one by falling into hands that could not appreciate them, and were allowed to be destroyed. The vestry no longer performed its function of "visiting" them, and possibly the the rectors no longer stood in dread of suit if they neglected the charge. There are many volumes in existence, and every now and then an old book comes to light from its hiding place in some out of the way garret. Some are still safe in the library of St. John's College, Annapolis, but in all other places, the folios, quartoes, and octavos are things of the past with but little superior to them to take their place.

The world has been a good deal disturbed within the last twenty five years upon the subject of altar cloths, they being regarded as emblematical of false and strange doctrine, just like the surplice was regarded as a "rag of popery." But like as in the matter of the surplice, the church in adopting altar cloths only went back to old things. For in 1791 we find in St. James' parish that "Dr. Claggett reported to this vestry that the vestry of All Saints' Parish, Calvert Co., had three yards of purple broadcloth for sale, which he thought would suit for a communion cloth, and hangings for the pulpit in this parish church, and that the price of the same was one guinea a yard. The vestry directed the doctor to purchase the same." Nor was it only in that kind of embellishment, for we find a church in Prince George's County adorned with a painting over the Holy Table. Our views doubtless have expanded beyond theirs, and ornamentation is developed in a way that would make them wonder could their eyes be opened in one of our modern temples; but the root of the matter was there in very distinct form. Also we hear of a few organs, and one parish in 1763 levied two thousand pounds of tobacco to pay the organist.

The church in Maryland has almost entirely lost her hold upon the colored people. In some of the more out of the way parts of the state they are still found to attend her services, especially upon notable occasions, and in some places, though very few, chapels have been erected for them. But in all districts nearer the great centers where they are in frequent intercourse with the people of the cities, their ambition seems to have been excited, and now for many years, since long before their emancipation, they have withdrawn from the church entirely. They desired to have their own institutions, to regulate their own concerns, may be to gratify their emotional temperament, and their masters gave them leave.

During the colonial period, however, and afterwards this was not so, but the slave knelt at the same table with his master. In St. James' Parish in 1790 we find Dr. Claggett giving a list of the communicants, and out of the total of sixty-one we find thirteen "Black Brethren;" and in 1791 we find the same "Black Communicants" applying to the vestry for a "piece of ground on the church glebe adjoining the northeast corner of the church-yard, for a burying place for the said blacks and their descendants," which was granted. This may be to many a revelation of the condition of the slave at that time in Maryland. Appended to the list of communicants as thus given, is the following note: "Our worthy brethren, Edward Tillard and Walter Watson, members of our society and other congregations, were present and communicated with us this day."

Dr. Claggett's rectorship of St. James' was a great blessing to the parish by the force of the same qualities that afterward made his episcopate a blessing to the diocese of Maryland. A strong, vigorous intellect and clear common sense always distinguished him, and fitted him in the eyes of all that came in contact with him, for leadership. His interest, too, in everything that concerned the welfare of the church in the commonwealth at large, had early been manifested, and his thoughtful attention to these things is nowhere so strikingly exemplied as in the records of the parish over whose counsels he presided and whose deliberations he guided. His forecast also of the future needs of his diocese, is seen in the impression which doubtless he created in the vestry, of the necessity for more than one Bishop for Maryland. This was in 1790 when after the convention held that year in Easton, the ministers and church wardens were admitted to seats in the vestry. The effect also of his rectorship was permanent; for from his day the parish was marked by a deep active interest in all that concerned the church's welfare.

It is painful, however, to remember that the church's greatest depression had not been reached when he assumed the episcopate in 1792, either in his old parish or in the diocese at large. Maryland was to see darker days than even these. The diocese, notwithstanding his labors, was to decline in its clerical force, doubtless because in all the parishes the ability of the people to support the holy work declined. They were hours of sadness, and anxiety about existence; while also as an active cause of depression, the great Methodist movement that began at this time to show the elements of its vigorous power, carried off some of the choicer spirits among even the more influential people, together with a large part of the multitudinous poor who had never been taught to love the church. The schism was the more easily accomplished because church principles had never been duly understood, and because, it is to be feared, the memory of the old slanders was in too many instances sedulously fostered.

Between his death, however, in 1816 and this present time, a period that one life spans, what mighty changes have been wrought in Maryland and throughout the land. The little one has become a thousand and the small one a strong nation. The Lord has hastened it in his time. For there is still living one, and there have but recently passed away several, who remember Bishop Claggett's venerable form and appearance, especially on that solemn day when he returned to his old parish to minister for the last time, and when the mortal illness seized him that soon secured for him his eternal rest.

The old parish of St. James, doubtless a type of many in Maryland, is truly crowded with sacred memories, that hang about the sanctuary where holy men have ministered and holy saints have in their hearts and with their voices communed, and that hang no less about the habitations of the dead that encompass the sanctuary. For it was a fine thought and a sacred desire that made our fathers in the long time past choose the church yard where their remains might lie. When the Angel of God comes to call this children home, and the earth yields up its dead, there will be no place so fitting for that waking hour as that spot where in the flesh our incense of prayer and praise had ascended up on high.

AUTHORITIES USED.

Original Records of St. James Parish, A. A. Co.
Maryland Mss. from Archives of Fulham.
Gov. Sharpe's letters in Ms. (copy.)
Character of the province of Maryland, Alsop.
Early Friends in Maryland, Norris.
Life of Geo. Fox, vol. II.
Anderson's Colonial Church History.
Records of Piscataway parish, Md.
Eddis' Letters.
Grahame's Colonial History of the U. S.
Bancroft's History of U. S.
Parish Histories in Ms. Dr. Allen.
History St. Anne's parish, Dr. Allen.
History of Maryland, Dr. Allen.
Hawk's Ecclesiastical Contributions, vol. II.
History of Maryland, McMahon.
History of Maryland, Bozman.
Founders of Maryland, Neill.
The Foundation of Maryland, Gen. B. T. Johnson.
Narrative of a voyage to Maryland, Father White.
Records of the English Province, S. J. Md. letters.
Laws of Maryland, Bacon.
Archives of Maryland, Md. His. Soc.
History of the Church of England, Perry.

Protestant Episcopal Church in U. S. of A. Spencer.
Short's History of the Church of England.
Ranke's History of the Popes.
The Huguenots in France after the Revocation, Smiles.
Short History of the English People, Green.
History of England, Macauley.
History of England, Knight.
The Lords Baltimore, Morris.
Notes on Virginia Colonial Clergy, Neill.
Wenlock, Chistison, &c., Sam. Harrison.
Historical Sermon, Rev. W. C. Butler.
Oration of Gen. Charles E. Phelps, Baltimore's one hundred and fiftieth anniversary.
Parish Institutions of Maryland, E. Ingle.
Early Journals of the conventions of Maryland.
Articles on early American church history, J. V. Lewis, D. D.
Life of Bishop Claggett, J. N. Norton, D. D.
John Adams the Statesman of the American Revolution, Hon. M. Chamberlain.

CONTENTS.

Act concerning Religion,—6—112.
Architecture in the colony,—68.
Anne, Queen,—129.
Alms-basin,—170.
Adorning the altar,—170.
Adams, Rev. Alex.—256.
Allen, Rev. B.—262.
Additional Constitutions,—299.
Altar-cloth,—304.

Baptism of Slaves,—28.
Bray, Rev. Dr.—52.
Bishop, efforts to secure,—52—81—242—267.
Boundaries of St. James Parish,—63.
Bertrand, Rev. Paul,—67.
Butler, Bishop,—136.
Baltimore, Lord, the colony restored to,—143.
Blasphemy, law of 1723,—113—167.
Bacon, Rev. Thomas,—179.
Bachelors taxed,—210—234.
Boston, sufferers by fire in,—45—221.
Boucher, Rev. Mr,—229—251.

Conditions of Plantation,—12.

CONTENTS.

Coode, Rev. John,—12.
Camisards,—22.—
Convict emigrants,—38—127—207.
Copley, Gov.,—48.
Commissary, office of,—52.
Chapels of Ease,—56.
Constables,—75.
Counters of tobacco,—101.
Commutation of currency,—101.
Convocation suspended,—130.
Clergy, their condition in England,—132.
" their social status,—133.
" of Maryland, supporters of prerogative,—153.
Church Missionary Society,—141.
Colebatch, Rev. Mr.,—153.
Charles, the sixth Lord Baltimore,—155.
Ceremonial in Va., in 1724,—166.
Communicants,—185.
Chase, Rev. Mr.—187.
Cohabiting,—195.
Chandler, Rev. Dr.,—216.
Coventry parish,—216.
Clergy forbidden to assemble,—218—245.
Churches built,—228.
Contract for St. James' church,—230.
Claggett, Rev. Dr.,—284—285—304.
Convention, annual meeting of,—298.

Division of parishes,—56—99—148.
Donations,—94.
Difficulties between clergy and laity,—98.
Ducking-stool,—122.
Dulany, Dan.,—217.
Donatives, parishes said to be,—243.
Declaration of Rights.—254.

Endowments, church,—12.

CONTENTS.

Establishment of the church,—18.
" Act of,—24—154—248.
" good effects wrought out by,—33
Ecclesiastical court,—80—154—244—299.
Enquiries of 1717,—87—165.
Evangelical school,—137.
Education in the colony,—163.

Fires, none in churches,—120—197.
Free schools,—163.
French war, effects of,—207.
French Canadians,—211.
Frederick, Lord Baltimore,—212—267.
Fundamental rights and liberties,—287.
Fundamental principles,—291

Glebes,—94—95.
Gibson, Bishop of London,—181.

Hammond,—10.
Herring Creek parish,—67.
Hall, Rev. Henry,—77.
Hart, Governor,—81.
Henderson, Rev. Jacob,—85—155.

Induction, forms of,—77—158—159—188—262—266.
Interlocutory Judgment of Council,—192.
Intruders punished,—258.

Jesuit Fathers, Records of,—9—13.
" " Take up lands,—11.
" Missionaries,—143
Jones, Rev. Hugh,—71—166.

Kent Island, Settlement of,—8.
Kidnapping,—39.

Labadists,—45.
Libraries, Parish,—53—91—95—303.

CONTENTS.

London's, Bishop of, Authority,—79.
Library of St. James' Parish,—104.
Liquor, use of,—123.
Lang, Rev. John,—188—202.
Lake, Rev. Charles,—223—235.
Laity in Church Conventions,—296.

More, Henry,—9.
Mechanics in the Colony,—71.
Mulatto Children, Property of the Clergy,—72—125.
Money From Sale of Mulatto Children and Mothers,—72.
Methodists,—137.
Magowan, Rev. Walter,—260.

Negroes, not Baptized,—162.
" Disturb the White People at Church,—198
" Communicants,—199—305.

Organization of the Parish,—61.
Oaths taken by Vestrymen,—64—224—276.
Ogle, Governor,—184—223.
Offertory,—194.
Ordainers to the Ministry,—286.

Protestant Catholics,—9.
Population,—15—35—124—185.
Protestant Revolution,—15.
Popish Plot,—22.
Puritans,—41.
Pulpit Cushion,—73.
Pew Locks,—74.
Priests, Roman, Good Influence of,—127.
Plate, Inventory of,—203.
Proclamation act,—241.
Parishes at the Revolution,—250—256.
Petition to the Legislature in 1780,—280.

Quakers, Population,—23—42.

CONTENTS.

Quakers of Pennsylvania, Missionary to be sent to,—58.
" Good Influence of,—127.
" Descendants of, Indemnified in Mass.,—140.
" Spirit of,—144.

Revolt of 1681,—14.
Revocation of Edict of Nantes,—14—21.
Repairs on Churches, tax for,—102.
Ratio of Protestants to Roman Catholics,—40.
Roman Catholics, Treatment of,—114—116—209.

Slaves in Maryland,—28.
Settlers in Maryland, from whence,—36.
" Majority of the first Protestant,—40.
Slave Trade,—39—177.
School System of 1696,—51.
Service, Silver Communion,—73.
Seymour, Governor,—80.
Scepticism in the Colony,—93—167—180.
Sabbath Breaking,—113.
Stocks and Whipping Post,—114—196—233.
Stole and Surplice,—126—166—234.
Secker, Archbishop,—132—206.
Swift, Dean,—133.
Society for Propagating the Gospel,—141.
Salaries, Reduction of,—149—215.
School Master for Sale,—165.
Sharpe, Governor,—213—221—243.
Select Vestries, 275.
Standing Committee,—297—300.
Superintending Committee,—302.

Toleration in 1648,—10.
Toleration, English Act of,—26.
Taney, Mary,—13.
Taxables,—28.
Tobacco, its Varying Price,—56.

CONTENTS.

Tobacco, Amount Limited,--169.
Talbot and Welton, Bishops, in Maryland,--156.
Tustian, Rev. Peter,--158.
Tindal,--179.
Terret's, Nicholas, will,--200.

Urquhart, Rev. John,--171.

Vestry, Functions of,--29,
" Fined,--170.
" Ordered to Report to Council,--194.
" Act Agitation,--248.
Visitation, Dr. Bray's, at Annapolis,--57.
Violence Toward Clergy,--154.

Whites's Father, Narrative,--8.
Women, white with mulatto children,--71.
Walpole, Sir R.,--130.
Wesley, Rev. Sam.,--136.
Wesley, Rev. John and Charles,--136--177,
Whitfield,--136--177.
War, seven years,--204.
War, thirty years,--14.
White, Bishop,--302.

Yeo, Rev. John,--13.
Yale College, agitation on Episcopacy,--141.

www.ingramcontent.com/pod-product-compliance
Lightning Source LLC
Chambersburg PA
CBHW022042230426
43672CB00008B/1043